Intelligent Guide

The Southern Rh...

July 2018 edition

Benjamin Lewin MW
Copyright © 2018 Benjamin Lewin
ISBN: 9781976845475
Vendange Press
www.vendangepress.com

Without limiting the rights under copyright reserved above, no part of this publication may be reproduced, stored in or introduced into a retrieval system, or transmitted, in any form or by any means (electronic, mechanical, photocopying, recording or otherwise) without the prior written permission of both the copyright owner and the above publisher of the book. All enquiries should be directed to contact@vendangepress.com.

Preface

The first part of this guide discusses the Southern Rhône, and explains the character and range of its wines. The second part profiles the producers. There are detailed profiles of the leading producers, showing how each winemaker interprets the local character, and mini-profiles of other important estates. The *Guide to the Northern Rhône* applies the same approach to the region immediately to the north.

In the first part, I address the nature of the wines made today and ask how this has changed, how it's driven by tradition or competition, and how styles may evolve in the future. I show how the wines are related to the terroir and to the types of grape varieties that are grown, and I explain the classification system. For each region, I suggest reference wines that illustrate the character and variety of the area.

In the second part, there's no single definition for what constitutes a top producer. Leading producers range from those who are so prominent as to represent the common public face of an appellation to those who demonstrate an unexpected potential on a tiny scale. The producers profiled in the guide represent the best of both tradition and innovation in wine in the region. In each profile, I have tried to give a sense of the producer's aims for his wines, of the personality and philosophy behind them—to meet the person who makes the wine, as it were, as much as to review the wines themselves.

Each profile shows a sample label, a picture of the winery, and details of production, followed by a description of the producer and winemaker. Each producer is rated (from one to three stars). For each producer I suggest reference wines that are a good starting point for understanding the style. Most of the producers welcome visits, although some require appointments: details are in the profiles. Profiles are organized geographically, and each group of profiles is preceded by maps showing the locations of producers to help plan itineraries.

The guide is based on many visits to the region over recent years. I owe an enormous debt to the many producers who cooperated in this venture by engaging in discussion and opening innumerable bottles for tasting. This guide would not have been possible without them.

Benjamin Lewin

Contents

Overview of the Rhône	1
Appellations in the Southern Rhône	3
Châteauneuf-du-Pape	9
Special Cuvées	13
Climate Change and Alcohol	18
Gigondas & Vacqueyras	19
Beaumes de Venise & Others	24
Blending versus Cuvées	25
Vintages	26
Visiting the Region	27
Profiles of Leading Estates	30
Estates in Châteauneuf-du-Pape	31
Estates in Gigondas, Vacqueyras, & Beaumes de Venise	66
Estates in Côtes du Rhône	80
Ventoux & Luberon	96
Mini-Profiles of Important Estates	98
Glossary of French Wine Terms	114
Index of Estates by Rating	116
Index of Organic and Biodynamic Estates	117
Index of Estates by Appellation	118
Index of Estates by Name	120

Tables

Grape Varieties in Capsule	4
Appellations in Capsule	8
Reference Wines for Châteauneuf-du-Pape	14
Reference Wines for Southern Rhône Crus and Côtes	26

Appellation Maps

Southern Rhône	8
Châteauneuf-du-Pape	12
Gigondas, Vacqueyras, and Beaumes de Venise	21

Producer Maps

Symbols for Producers	30
Southern Rhône	31
Châteauneuf-du-Pape AOP	32
Châteauneuf-du-Pape Village	33
Gigondas, Vacqueyras, and Beaumes de Venise	66
Côtes du Rhône	80
Cairanne-Séguret	81

Overview of the Rhône

The river Rhône flows more or less directly south for 200 miles from Lyon to the Mediterranean, and is divided into two very different areas for winemaking. The Northern Rhône and Southern Rhône have little connection in terms of production, climate, or grape varieties. The Northern Rhône occupies a skinny band of vineyards along the river between Vienne (just south of Lyon) and Valence. Then there is a 30 mile gap before the start of the vineyards of the Southern Rhône; spreading out widely on both sides of the river, they extend all the way to Avignon.

The Southern Rhône is one of the major wine-producing areas of France in terms of quantity; by contrast, the Northern Rhône produces only about 5% of the quantity of the South. The Southern Rhône is divided between vast regional appellations, with the Côtes du Rhône as the largest, surrounded by a series of regional AOPs, similar in style but lesser in quality. A relatively small part of its production comes from smaller appellations, formally known as Crus. These are equivalent in quality to the appellations of the Northern Rhône.

Besides AOP production, wine is produced under the broad rubric of the IGP Méditerranée (or the departmental IGPs within it), which covers a wide swatch of the Rhône and Provence: most of it comes from the Ardèche (to the west of the Rhône) and the Vaucluse (stretching southeast from Avignon into Provence).

The southern Rhône is where the transition occurs to lush, fruit-driven wines. Most of the vineyards lie between Montélimar and Avignon. The south has a more Mediterranean climate than the northern Rhône, with more sunshine and less rainfall. The valley widens out and there is a variety of terrains, including alluvial deposits, sandy areas, and limestone.

The Northern and Southern Rhône are each relatively homogeneous in terms of climatic conditions. It's not uncommon for a vintage to be better in one rather than the other, but it would be unusual for different parts of either region to perform very differently in a particular vintage.

With a cooler climate, the Northern Rhône vineyards are based on Syrah, and the red wines are monovarietals. The whites, in a small minority, are often based on Marsanne and Roussanne. By contrast, the Southern Rhône has a much wider range of varieties, and most wines are blended from several varieties. Grenache is the predominant black

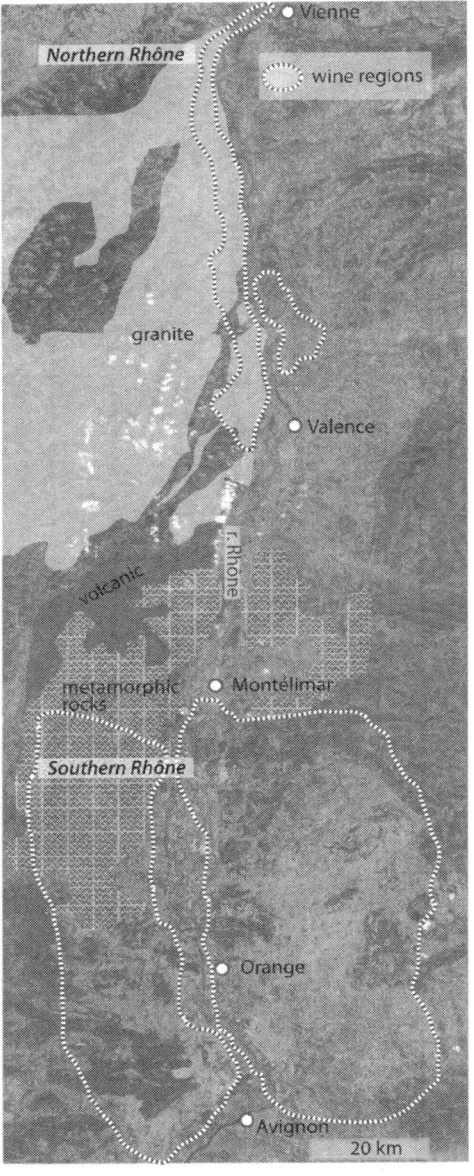

The river Rhône is the dividing line between metamorphic or volcanic rocks (to the west) and sedimentary rocks (to the east). Soils are sedimentary except as indicated. Vineyards of the Northern Rhône are north of Valence; vineyards of the Southern Rhône are south of Montélimar.

variety, giving the wines of the Southern Rhône their richer, more southern, impression, more alcoholic, and not usually long-lived.

The mix of the blend has been changing. The biggest change is an increase in Syrah from virtually nothing in the 1960s to 20% of the blend today. The trend is to wines that producers call GSM, shorthand for Grenache-Syrah-Mourvèdre, which now total three quarters of production. Grenache gives richness, Syrah brings some restraint, and Mourvèdre adds structure. Plantings of Cinsault, Counoise, and Carignan, none of which bring much to the blend, have been declining. Red is by the far the greatest part of production. Rosé comes next, largely from Grenache or Cinsault. The whites rarely reach the same level of interest as the reds. Most are made from Grenache Blanc and Clairette, neither really a high quality variety. Some white wines have Roussanne or Viognier.

There has been a great change in the Southern Rhône in the past ten or twenty years. The red wines used to have a certain heavy feeling, with rustic impressions from Côtes du Rhône becoming smoother going through the Crus from Vacqueyras to Gigondas to Châteauneuf-du Pape. Châteauneuf was unmistakably powerful. Producers never used words such as finesse and elegance, which I heard quite often on my most recent visit. Refinement has increased along the line.

Côtes du Rhône shows the widest variation, from simple wines for immediate consumption to quite serious wines, especially from named villages, that bear keeping for three or four years. Vacqueyras and Gigondas have broken out of their former rusticity. Châteauneuf-du Pape can be quite sleek, although its special cuvées still tend to be powerful and can be overwhelming when coming from very old Grenache. Whites used to have a heavy, somewhat phenolic impression, but today try to move towards freshness. The countervailing trend is the increase in alcohol; 14.5% or even 15% is the new 13.5%. My tasting notes often comment, "this is very good, but would be great if it had 1% less alcohol," since this would let the flavors show more clearly.

Appellations in the Southern Rhône

The Côtes du Rhône extends across the entire Southern Rhône, and accounts for almost two thirds of production. Surrounding the Côtes du Rhône are a series of regional appellations, which together account for a quarter of total production. The principles of production are similar to the Côtes du Rhône, focusing on improving the wine by specifying a minimum level of Grenache, but regulations are less stringent, and yields are higher. Producing pleasant, but generally undistinguished, country wines, the best known regional appellations are Ventoux (formerly the Côtes du Ventoux) and Grignan-les-Adhémar (formerly Coteaux du Tricastin, but with a recent name change to remove any connection to the nuclear power station at Tricastin).

Grape Varieties in Capsule

Red

Grenache is the workhorse grape of the south, responding well to high temperatures, but producing high alcohol at ripeness. It has a tendency to oxidation (so it is usually aged in cuve), turning to nutty flavors, and usually the wines are best enjoyed young. It's usually blended, but varietal wines are sometimes made from very old vines.

Syrah is relatively deeply colored with good tannins. Whereas in the northern Rhône it is usually vinified as a varietal, in the south it is a major quality component of the blend. It has a tendency to reduction and so is often aged in wood.

Mourvèdre is intensely colored and structured with strong tannins. A little goes a long way, and it brings structure to the blend. It's often aged in wood.

Cinsault is an old blending grape of the region, rather productive without much flavor unless yields are really suppressed. It's often used to make rosé.

Counoise is useful for adding acidity, but does not have much color or flavor.

Carignan is an old grape of the south (common in Languedoc), but it is rather characterless unless the vines are very old. It is limited to 30% in the Côtes du Rhône, but has largely been uprooted.

White

Clairette is one of the major workhorse varieties and tends to show light aromatics with an impression of citrus. It can be a strong majority of a blend or occasionally a monovarietal. It's becoming more popular because of its ability to retain acidity.

Bourboulenc is useful because it is a late-ripening variety. Often used as a blending grape, it's rare that it's a major focus.

Grenache Blanc tends to be rather nondescript, useful for filling out a blend, but rarely vinified by itself.

Marsanne is a workhorse grape of the Northern Rhône, but less common in the south, where its tendency to bitterness and high alcohol can be a problem.

Roussanne is the most refined grape variety of the Rhône. Vinified as a monovarietal, it has a tendency to develop a honeyed palate. As part of a blend, it brings elegance.

Other black varieties are Vaccarèse, Muscardin, and Terret Noir. Other whites are Picpoul, and Picardin.

Close to two thirds of Côtes du Rhône wines are made by cooperatives. Much of the rest is made by negociants; the negociants of the north—Guigal, Chapoutier, and Jaboulet—all have substantial production of Côtes du Rhône, as do negociants from the south, such as Perrin (who started at Château Beaucastel in Châteauneuf-du-Pape). Only a relatively small part of production comes from growers who make wine themselves. And many of the best wines come from small producers whose primary focus is wine from a smaller appellation, but who also have vineyards in the Côtes du Rhône. In fact, it's fascinating to see how far the style of the higher level appellation carries into the Côtes du Rhône in cases where a producer has vineyards in both. Some of the best Côtes du Rhône come from producers in Châteauneuf-du-Pape, for example. Few producers have built reputations on the Côtes du Rhône as such.

Côtes du Rhône is something of a catch-all. Not only can the wines be sourced from anywhere in the Rhône, either north or south (although as a practical matter almost all comes from the south) but there's wide variation in the composition of grape varieties. Nominally Grenache must be at least 40% (unless the wine comes from north of Montélimar), and Syrah and Mourvèdre must together be at least another 20%. However, producers will give you wines labeled Côtes du Rhône that they say are 100% Syrah or even 100% Mourvèdre. Granted that these are exceptions, there is still a wide range from wines that are soft and fruity to some that are more serious (often coming from vineyards adjacent to the Crus).

A scandal in 2018 erupted with the report that 15% of the Côtes du Rhône sold between 2013 and 2016 was fraudulent. This was not a result of widespread fraud, but was due to one large bulk-wine merchant, Raphaël Michel, who labeled table wine as Côtes du Rhône. Some Châteauneuf-du-Pape was also faked. The failure of the authorities to identify the merchant cast a pall over the whole region, but this should not discourage you from drinking Côtes du Rhône from other producers.

A superior level of wine, the Côtes du Rhône Villages, was created in 1953. Today it occupies about a quarter of the area of the Côtes du Rhône. About half of the village areas are allowed to label the wine with the name of the individual village. The main differentiating factor in the quality of the village wine is that the minimum proportion of Grenache is increased to at least 50%. Yields become progressively lower going from Côtes du Rhône to Côtes du Rhône Villages, to the individual villages. And wine from the Villages tends to be made by

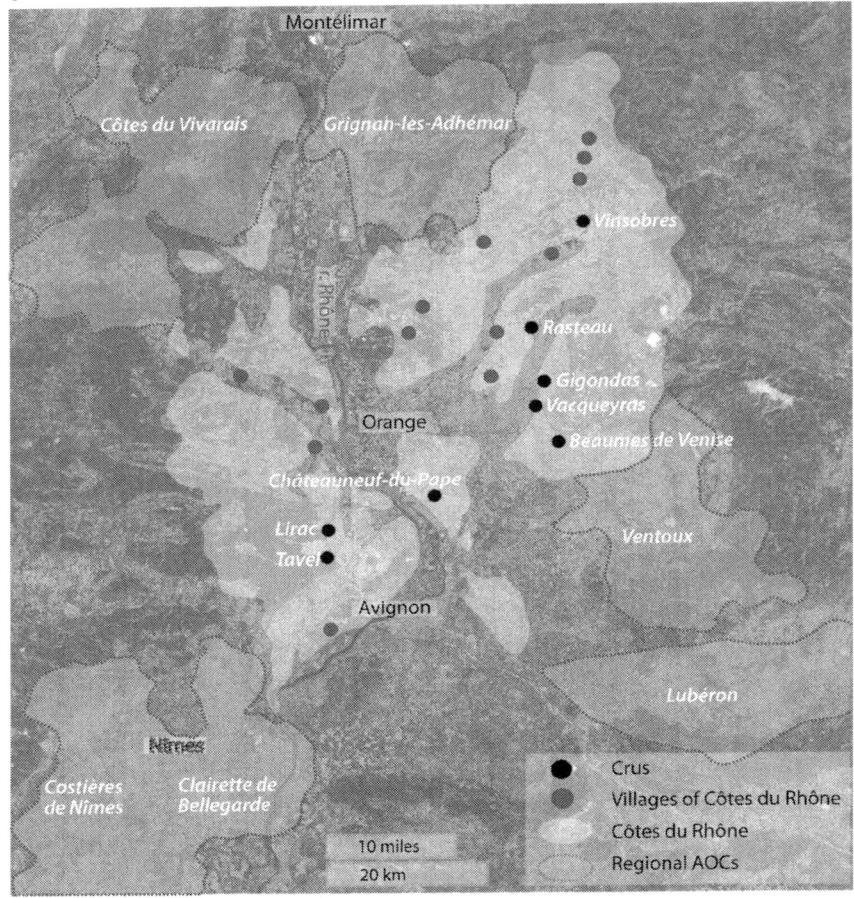

The Côtes du Rhône occupy most of the southern Rhône. They are surrounded by other regional appellations. Within them are the individual villages of the Côtes du Rhône Villages and the "Crus" (individual appellations).

conventional vinification, whereas there is a more of a tendency in Côtes du Rhône to use carbonic maceration, the technique pioneered in Beaujolais to produce a simple, forward, fruity wine.

The individual appellations are officially called the "Crus" of the Côtes du Rhône. Each has its own rules and regulations. The first, and by far the best known, is Châteauneuf-du-Pape, which was there at the very creation of the AOC system. Lirac and Tavel are also long established as AOPs. Most of the appellations in the Southern Rhône allow production of red, rosé, or white wine (although red wine is always in

Appellations in Capsule

Appellation	Annual Bottles	Type
Côtes du Rhône (62%)		
Côtes du Rhône	200 million	81% red
Côtes du Rhône Villages	45 million	88% red
Regional appellations (25%)		
Costières de Nîmes	29 million	52% red
Vivarais + Duché d'Uzes	3 million	53% red
Grignan les Adhémar	9 million	76% red
Luberon	21 million	46% red
Ventoux	36 million	68% red
"Old" Crus (9%)		
Châteauneuf-du-Pape	13 million	93% red
Gigondas	5 million	99% red
Lirac	3 million	87% red
Vacqueyras	6 million	95% red
Tavel	5 million	100% rosé
VDN Muscat de Beaumes de Venise	1 million	100% fortified
Recent Crus (4%)		
Beaumes de Venise	3 million	100% red
Cairanne	4 million	96% red
Rasteau	4.5 million	100% red
Vinsobres	2.6 million	100% red

The Côtes du Rhône and the Crus produce mostly red wine, except for Tavel (rosé) and VDN (fortified) from Beaumes de Venise and Rasteau. The surrounding regional appellations mostly produce rosé as well as red.

a strong majority, and sometimes white is not allowed), but Tavel is an exception that makes only rosé, and Beaumes de Venise and Rasteau are best known for their fortified sweet dessert wines.

Some villages have been promoted out of the Côtes du Rhône Villages to become appellations in their own right. The first was Gigondas in 1971, followed by Vacqueyras in 1990, then Vinsobres in 2007 and Cairanne in 2015. Some of the historical changes in status can be confusing. Beaumes de Venise has been an AOP for sweet, fortified white wine made from the Muscat grape since 1945. But it was also part of the Côtes du Rhône Villages for red wine production, and became a named village in 1978. Then in 2005 Beaumes de Venise became an appellation for red wine production. Rasteau has a similar history. The detailed characterizations and changes in status seem positively theological (very appropriate for an area that once hosted the Papacy).

The mix of grape varieties is similar across the Southern Rhône; the only really significant difference between appellations is just how strongly Grenache dominates. So what is responsible for differences in character—terroir? climate? historical accidents? I suppose it's a throwback that alcohol level increases along the hierarchy of appellations or cuvées: in 2010, Côtes du Rhône (including Villages and named villages) averaged 14.2%, Gigondas was 14.5%, Châteauneuf-du-Pape was 14.7%, and the Châteauneuf-du-Pape prestige cuvées were 14.9%. This goes back to the time when there was a struggle to reach ripeness, which was taken as a marker for quality. But while more alcohol may have been better then, it is a problem today.

The dividing line in expectations of quality comes when the label has an individual place name. "People call the villages of the Côtes du Rhône Villages by name as though they were Crus. They think the big difference comes between the Côtes du Rhône and Côtes du Rhône Villages on the one hand, versus the individual village names and the Crus on the other. The villages with names and the crus are very close today," says Christian Voeux, who made wine at Château La Nerthe in Châteauneuf-du-Pape and also at his Domaine d'Amauve in Séguret. This view is certainly reinforced when you look at the labels: the village name is the most prominent feature whether the wine is from a named village or a cru, and you would have to look carefully at the small type underneath to determine the difference.

How important are the differences between places? "There's a range of vineyards in Séguret, Sablet, and Gigondas from the Coteaux to the high slopes, but differences among the wines are due less to the terroir than to the style of each producer," says Christian Voeux, although the villages have different (and better) exposures than the plain of the Côtes du Rhône as a whole. In horizontal tastings of the Côtes du Rhône, it seems to me that there is usually a step up in quality, showing as greater concentration, going from Côtes du Rhône to Côtes du Rhône Villages. I do not actually sense any further increase moving on to the named villages, nor do I see any specific characteristics that consistently distinguish one village from another (perhaps Sablet gives the finest impression).

There are negociant wines that seem well made but uninteresting (you feel you might be able to pick out the wines of the big negociants in a blind tasting for their squeaky clean impression), wines from independent producers that are aimed at the market for immediate gratification on the basis of simple, forward, fruits, and wines that are more "serious" with enough structure to improve for a year or so. Perhaps there are more in the last category when the village is named, but the producer's name needs to be the guide here. At all events, the issue in choosing a Côtes du Rhône is style and quality, rather than expression of terroir. What happens when we move on to the 'Crus'?

Châteauneuf-du-Pape

There is little dispute that the best red wines of the Southern Rhône come from Châteauneuf-du-Pape, which has produced wine for centuries. Châteauneuf-du-Pape has always been blended from many grape varieties, but the varieties have changed over time. Today's dominant variety, Grenache, was introduced in the 1820s. The result was "a more generous, full-bodied wine with a deeper color, but less elegance."

At first, the trend to richer wines was resisted in Châteauneuf-du-Pape. After phylloxera, when Joseph Duclos led the replanting at Château La Nerthe, he recommended a maximum of 20% of Grenache and Cinsault (and a minimum of 10% of white grapes). By the late 1930s, Baron Le Roy de Boiseaumarié of Château Fortia, who was instrumental in making Châteauneuf-du-Pape one of the first appellation contrôlées (in 1936), was denouncing producers who had made their wines rich and heavy with Grenache.

There's a reasonable case for saying that today the best Grenache-based wines in the world come from Châteauneuf-du-Pape, although there are some regions in Spain that might challenge the claim. "Châteauneuf is a marriage between the worst soil in the world and Grenache," says Daniel Brunier of Domaine du Vieux Télégraphe.

The impetus for planting Grenache, however, may have been only partly connected with the character of Châteauneuf-du-Pape. Through the 1920s, growers in Châteauneuf-du-Pape were encouraged to produce Grenache because they got twice the price for selling it to "improve" Burgundy than they could get for other varieties. Presumably the Grenache went into Châteauneuf-du-Pape after the AOP regulations stopped it being exported to Burgundy in the 1930s. Grenache became so dominant in the southern Rhône in the 1960s that INAO advised growers to "cool the ardor of the Grenache" by planting Cinsault—pretty terrible advice that, when accepted, led to dilution in the wine. Reducing Grenache was not a bad idea, but Cinsault was not the right substitute. By the nineties, there was a move away from Grenache; today it has fallen to around 72%.

The regulations for the AOP limit the grape varieties that can be grown, but not their proportions. It's usually said that thirteen varieties are permitted, but actually the total is fourteen because Grenache (Noir) and Grenache Blanc are counted as one variety. The total includes nine black varieties and five white varieties. However, almost all production (more than 90%) is red. Most Châteauneuf-du-Pape is blended, although it is now rare for all of the permitted varieties to be used; Château Beaucastel and Domaine de Beaurenard are holdouts that insist on including at least a small amount of every variety.

After Grenache became the predominant grape variety, fashions changed regarding other varieties. After the debacle with Cinsault, Syrah became popular in the 1970s; today it is the second most planted variety, although it still amounts to only 11%. Mourvèdre is next at 7%. Cinsault is reduced today to a mere 2.5%. So a typical red Châteauneuf is full bodied, with forward fruits coming from the predominant Grenache, structure and aromatics from Syrah, and tannins from Mourvèdre. The proportions of Cinsault, Counoise, Vaccarèse, and Muscardin have been decreasing, and the other varieties are hardly used at all. For practical purposes, the average red Châteauneuf today is a classic GSM blend of up to three quarters Grenache supported by Syrah and Mourvèdre.

A tendency to produce more single vineyard wines makes the blend less predictable. Indeed, many single vineyard wines also come from single varietals, most often Grenache, but sometimes Mourvèdre. I have not encountered any monovarietal Syrahs. In whites, the varietals that may make monovarietals are most often Clairette or Roussanne.

For whites, Grenache Blanc and Clairette tend to be dominant components in blends, with lesser amounts of Roussanne and Bourboulenc. The highest quality variety by far is Roussanne, and it achieves its heights in the Vieilles Vignes monovarietal Roussanne bottling from Château Beaucastel. Clairette is becoming more popular because of its

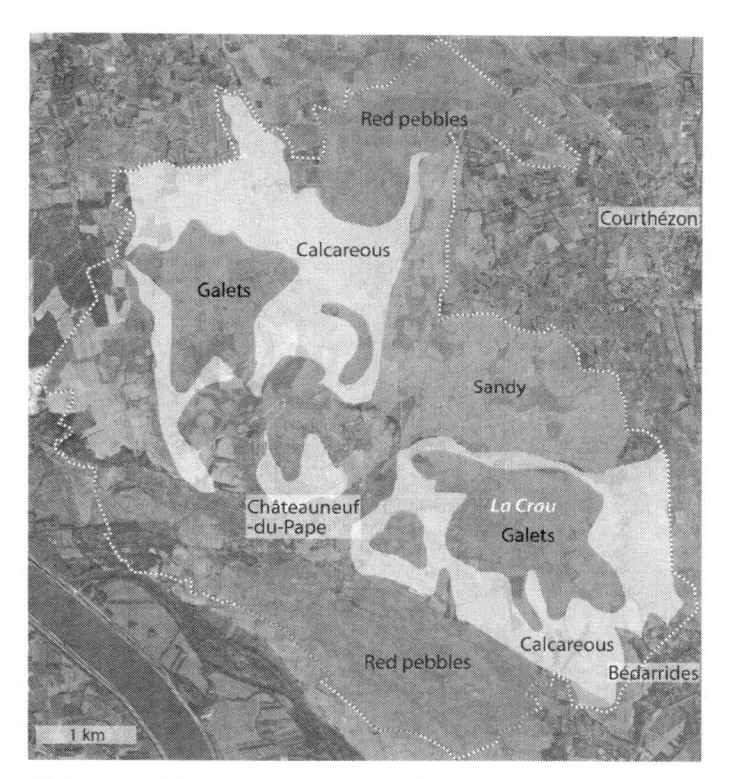

Châteauneuf-du-Pape has a variety of terroirs.

ability to retain acidity, and it certainly freshens a blend; the issue is to get full flavor variety. Of course, there are always exceptions: although Château Rayas is most famous by far for its red wine, the white, coming from a blend of Grenache Blanc and Clairette, offers a wonderful savory representation of the garrigue.

Whites are only 7% of production in Châteauneuf-du-Pape, but slowly there's more focus on producing wines with good freshness. "Many producers in Châteauneuf-du-Pape really do red—the white is just on the side. It's a pity because we have the potential for producing great whites. The problem in the south is to keep freshness and acidity, but our whites are actually more consistent than the reds across vintages. If you do it properly, I am sure we can compete with great white Burgundies," says Florent Lançon at Domaine de la Solitude.

The tradition in Châteauneuf is to blend both grape varieties and terroirs. Terroir is an interesting issue, as the size of the appellation means there are several different sectors. Soils range from calcareous in the

The galets (round stones) of Châteauneuf-du-Pape cover vineyards in the eastern part.

west, to sandy in the east, and to rocky in the south. Both to south and north, there are red soils, with iron-rich rocks and pebbles. The best known terroir consists of the famous *galets roulants*, rolling pebbles, most prominent on the plateau of La Crau in the southeast, but also found in the northwest. Their well-rounded shape reflects their origin in having been deposited by the Rhône.

The special quality of this terroir is often attributed to the fact that the galets absorb heat by day and reflect it back up at the vines at night. Now this is a curious contrast with the common view in most wine regions that diurnal variation is helpful because a cooling-off at night allows the vines a necessary respite from the heat of the day, and helps to retain acidity. Perhaps a more important attribute of the galets is that they form a barrier to evaporation, and therefore help to retain moisture in the soil in this dry climate.

It's curious that producers will discuss the characteristics of the various terroirs with regards to their effects on the character of the wine, including the advantages to be gained by an assemblage of lots from different terroirs, but I have never heard a producer express the idea that different grape varieties should be matched to the terroirs in Châteauneuf-du-Pape. Yet this is the first concern about terroir everywhere else in France. Châteauneuf producers are pragmatic about grape varieties, adjusting the mix in accordance with their stylistic preferences, but there appears to be no concentration of any specific variety on any

The "red soils" south of Châteauneuf-du-Pape consist of ferruginous pebbles. Vines are pruned as individual bushes to withstand high winds.

specific terroir. If there's any distinction, it is simply in choosing whether black or white varieties are the most appropriate for a plot. Many producers make Côtes du Rhône as well as Châteauneuf-du-Pape, but this usually comes from different vineyards, often just outside the appellation (sometimes even contiguous with the producer's vineyards within Châteauneuf-du-Pape). Nominally it is forbidden to declassify Châteauneuf-du-Pape to Côtes du Rhône, so deselecting a lot requires it to become IGP or Vin de France. So you should be cautious when you see a Côtes du Rhône described as declassified Châteauneuf-du-Pape.

Special Cuvées

Châteauneuf producers divide their wines into two categories. The first group is "traditional;" the second group is described as the special cuvées, or just the "cuvées." "Traditional" refers to the way the wine was blended, and doesn't necessarily carry any stylistic implication. Sometimes the "traditional" wine is in the old style of Châteauneuf, but sometimes it's a more modern take. "For traditional cuvées, the tendency is to make a blend from different terroirs; single terroirs are processed separately only for the special cuvées," explains Michel Blanc of the producers' association. "Châteauneuf-du-Pape is a blend, it's interesting to make a vinification of a special terroir for a special

Reference Wines for Châteauneuf-du-Pape

Red

Château Rayas	100% Grenache
Château Beaucastel	All 13 varieties
Château La Nerthe	GSM
Bosquet des Papes	GSM
Domaine du Vieux Télégraphe	GSM + Cinsault, Clairette
Paul Autard, La Côte Ronde	50% Grenache, 50% Syrah

White

Château Rayas	50% Grenache, 50% Clairette
Chante Perdrix, Etienne Pecoul	100% Clairette
Domaine Saint Préfert	15% Clairette, 85% Roussanne
Domaine de la Solitude, Barberini	80% Roussanne, 20% Clairette
Château de la Gardine, Marie Léoncie	90% Roussanne, 10% Clairette
Château Beaucastel, Vieilles Vignes	100% Roussanne

case, but it should not become a majority of production," he believes. Some of the special cuvées come from old vines (these are often very old, going back to the first replanting after phylloxera).

The traditional position was expressed by Sophie Armenier at Domaine de Marcoux when I asked her view of special cuvées. "I don't believe in them. Well, everyone can do what they want, of course. I think that the strength of Châteauneuf is diversity, the different results coming from the cépages and the terroir, and if I made cuvées from each sector, one year the south would be good, another year a different area. The most interesting wine is made by assemblage." Of course, it's an open question what effect it will have on the regular Châteauneuf-du-Pape to put the best selections into special cuvées. With more than a hundred producers now offering special cuvées, so that today they amount to almost 10% of production, can the remaining 90% of Châteauneuf-du-Pape withstand the loss?

Relatively few wines show the thick, jammy character that might have been associated with Châteauneuf a decade or more ago. Many wines are strongly fruit-driven, but a surprising number are more structured, and show refined palates with some tautness to the tannins and underlying structure. A tendency towards high-toned aromatics, however, is common with warmer vintages. My general impression is that Châteauneuf would be a more interesting wine—and a better match for food—if producers pulled back a bit further on the Grenache.

The cuvées tend to be more powerful. You reach a point at which it's difficult to distinguish them: one cult wine at this level looks much like another, irrespective of origin, irrespective of grape variety. Part of the extra concentration of the special cuvées is because many come from low-yielding old vines, so they tend to be Grenache, as this is the predominant variety in really old vines.

I am not at all sure that cuvées of 100% Grenache are the best way to go for the region. I would say Châteauneuf is quite aromatic enough without needing to go any further in the direction of über-Châteauneufs. Admitting that the special cuvées are impressive in terms of power and intensity, I might prefer a traditional Châteauneuf for dinner, especially if it is in the more elegant (modern) style. And along with greater concentration, the cuvées tend to have more alcohol.

There's also a tendency with some of the special cuvées to use new oak barriques. The tradition in Châteauneuf is to mature red wine in foudres—very large wooden casks, usually of old oak. Demi-muids (600 liter) casks, are also used. The high ratio of volume to surface area reduces exposure to oxygen; foudres are favored because Grenache is an oxidative variety, prone to spoil if exposed to too much oxygen. Some producers use barriques to mature Syrah (and sometimes Mourvèdre), because these varieties need more exposure to oxygen to counter their natural reductive tendencies. "Barriques are interesting for people who make Syrah and Mourvèdre separately, but we do assemblage first, so the wine is 70% Grenache when it's maturing," says Didier Negron, explaining why Domaine Roger Sabon uses the larger containers.

If any single factor is most responsible for changing the character of Châteauneuf-du-Pape, it's been the introduction of special cuvées. One of the holdouts for tradition is Domaine du Vieux Télégraphe, where Daniel Brunier has gone in the opposite direction, improving the quality of his regular cuvée by producing a second wine (Télégramme) from declassified lots. "I think the special cuvées did a lot for Châteauneuf-du-Pape," he says. "I mean a lot positive and a lot negative. The problem is that today people think a special cuvée has to be more: more tannin, more wood, it's terrible. It brings a lot because they tend to attract, they turn the light on Châteauneuf-du-Pape, that was good, but a negative point for me is that they tend to push the people to make wine for someone else, not for themselves. I am convinced that people who make fruit bombs do not serve this wine to their family."

The traditional foudres—wooden casks of around 4,500 liters—are stacked along the sides of the cellar at Château Beaucastel. There are some 225 liter barriques in the center.

Increasing alcohol levels are part of the reason for a recent move away from Grenache towards Syrah and Mourvèdre. Grenache's tendency to high alcohol is enhanced when the growing season is shortened by higher temperatures. "Today we are convinced that Grenache is ripe only when it is very ripe—the Grenache *really* needs to be ripe to get concentration," says Daniel Brunier.

The trend towards Syrah has been strong, but may have run its course. "There were a lot of plantings of Syrah in the 1980s-1990s, but now this has stopped, because more than 15-20% in the blend changes the wine too much," says Michel Blanc. "Our objective here is the same as elsewhere, to have the same alcoholic and phenolic maturity; perhaps we should have more Mourvèdre," he says.

Indeed there's a move to Mourvèdre, but it's still only a small proportion of plantings. "In the past thirty years we have increased Mourvèdre; originally it was only 5%. But it's not so easy, you have to decide to pull out some vines. We wanted to have more definition of tannins and potential for aging. The Mourvèdre can be black and dense compared with Grenache, which is too nice, too round," says Daniel Brunier.

The great advocate for Mourvèdre has always been Château Beaucastel, which was quite controversial through the 1980s and 1990s because of the presence of Brett in its wine. (Brett is caused by the spoilage yeast Brettanomyces and gives an earthy, leathery note to the

From these old cellars at Château Rayas comes one of the best wines of Châteauneuf-du-Pape.

wine; the problem is that while a small amount can add complexity, it's erratic, and can easily reach a level at which it spoils the wine.) They believe at Beaucastel that people may have confused Brett with the natural animal quality of Mourvèdre; but all the same, in the late nineties they renovated the cellars to eliminate Brett. Personally I'm somewhat inclined to wonder whether the fruits of Châteauneuf-du-Pape aren't so overpowering, that a touch of something to take off the edge is helpful in achieving complexity. Perhaps this is just the modern trend, but for whatever reason, Beaucastel's wines today seem to have come more into the mainstream (meaning fruit-driven) of Châteauneuf-du-Pape. I can't help but feel slightly regretful about this, although anyone who feels that any Brett is an unacceptable contamination of the purity of fruits will disagree with me.

Showing that there is an infinite variety of ways to make great wine, another renowned producer, Château Rayas, makes its Châteauneuf-du-Pape exclusively from Grenache. Château Rayas has always been an odd man out, with eccentric proprietors who marched only to the beat of their own drum. I still have in my cellar an old vintage of Rayas with a label that says "Premier Grand Cru," a term that is very definitely not legal in Châteauneuf-du-Pape.

On a recent visit, Château Rayas lived up to its reputation for having dilapidated cellars. Aside from the fermentation cuves, everything is old wood, very old wood in fact, in various sizes from barriques or tonneaux to larger containers. I asked Emmanuel Reynaud, the proprietor, if he ever uses any new oak. "Why would I want to do that," he said with a look of amazement. "I make wine," he added as a further (self-evident) explanation.

Climate Change and Alcohol

High alcohol levels remain my main concern about Châteauneuf-du-Pape today. The wines have always tended to be alcoholic, easily achieving 12.5-13% alcohol in mid twentieth century. A level of 13.5% towards the end of the century was part of the richness of the style. But today it is usually higher. In fact, "I think it's difficult to make a good Châteauneuf under 14.5% alcohol," says Sophie Armenier at Domaine de Marcoux.

Producers have a variety of views about the current trend. "For us the alcohol content is the same since the beginning. When you get to 15.5% alcohol but you have no taste of alcohol, you have minerality and saltiness—it's magic," says Daniel Brunier. "The increase in alcohol is difficult to manage because it's just coming from the sun," says Michel Blanc at the Fédération. "You have to choose between alcohol and maturity. It's a matter of one or two days. If you are a day too late, the alcohol is a per cent higher," says Fabrice Brunel at Les Cailloux. Producers realize that consumers can be wary of high alcohol levels. "This is 16.5% alcohol," said one producer as we tasted a red Châteauneuf, "but I'll label it as 15%, so it will be fine."

The consensus, insofar as there is one, is that so far the situation has been manageable; but it will be difficult if the trend continues. I think this is optimistic: when alcohol exceeds 15%, it has (in my opinion) gone over the top. Even if it's not an overt presence on the palate when tasting, it's fatiguing when you try to drink a bottle. It's unclear how far a move away from Grenache might help without involving a significant change in style. The situation may be more serious in lesser appellations, where there tends to be less fruit concentration to balance the alcohol.

So what does global warming mean for Châteauneuf-du-Pape? "Today it is helping to make superb wines. Since 1999 the quality of our wines has increased. But if it continues for another 20 years we may have a problem, but there are grape varieties we do not use very much, like Counoise that do not develop high alcohol, so we could use more of them," says Christian Voeux at Château La Nerthe. So far so good. "The biggest effect of global warming is that we harvest earlier," says Daniel Brunier. "My concern with global warming is not the temperature, it is that if we don't have rain, then there will be a problem. Soil that needs to be irrigated is not called a terroir; it's just a soil, it has no interest for us."

Michel Chapoutier created a furor when he raised the issue of trying to deal with increasing alcohol: "The southern Rhône is too warm for Syrah. Of course we don't want to reduce the alcohol by physical means. If you use reverse osmosis to reduce the alcohol, you sacrifice some of the aromas. When you physically concentrate the grape must, you concentrate everything—including less desirable aspects. So how about simply adding back the water lost by evaporation? If you harvest on the basis of the ripeness of tannins in Grenache you risk having wines at 15.5 or 16% alcohol at least. We experimented and found that adding water did actually result in better wines. Wines with 17% alcohol just don't make sense. Lots of winemakers do it [adding water], and I think we should make it legal and bring it out in the open. It's the future of wine. We can't make Châteauneuf with 16% alcohol. We must have the courage to defend this point of view."

Gigondas & Vacqueyras

The most striking geological formation in the entire Southern Rhône is undoubtedly the Dentelles de Montmirail, a massive rock structure with a distinctly toothy appearance. The stark rocks loom over the village of Gigondas, and form the center of a semi circle of appellations: Gigondas, Vacqueyras, and Beaumes de Venise. Aside from Châteauneuf-du-Pape, these are the best known appellations on the east side of the river. They share the generally protective influence of the Dentelles, but the most direct effect is on Gigondas, where vineyards actually extend up the slopes of the mountain. The big difference here is not so much between appellations as between the plain and the slopes.

Gigondas is a very old area for wine—there's evidence of production in Roman times. Production was more or less halted by phylloxera, and the predominant crop became olives for the first half of the twentieth century. The great freeze of 1956 killed most of the olive trees, and then planting turned back to grapevines. The focus was heavily on Grenache, typically more than 90%, and the wine was known as the poor man's Châteauneuf-du-Pape. Gigondas had been part of the Côtes du Rhône when the appellation was created, and from 1951 was allowed to include the village name on the label; as

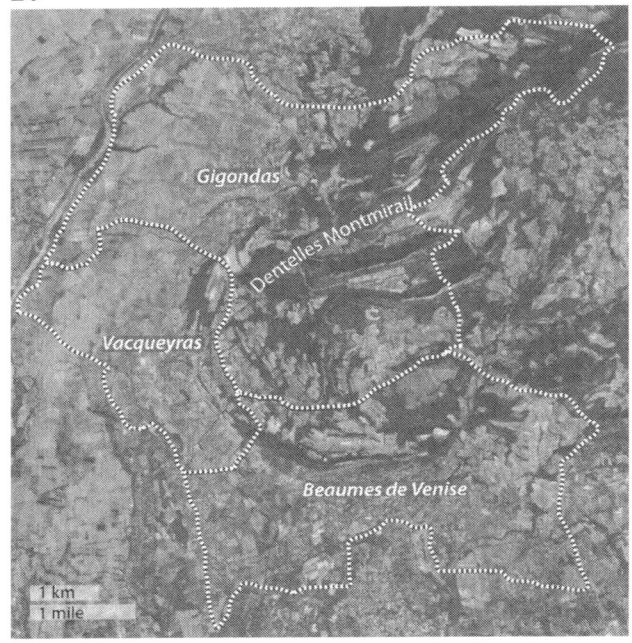

The appellations of Gigondas, Vacqueyras, and Beaumes de Venise form an arc around the Dentelles de Montmirail.

early as 1954, it began to agitate for its own appellation, but was rejected.

When it was finally approved in 1971, Gigondas became the fourth independent appellation in the region. The range of grape varieties was widened; current regulations limit Grenache to 80% and require a minimum of 15% of Syrah and/or Mourvèdre. The other varieties of the Côtes du Rhône, except Carignan, are also permitted. The most significant change was the inclusion of Syrah, which is regarded as introducing a more supple quality into wines that had been too hard.

Aside from one per cent of rosé, all production is red. Oak is not a big factor here: most vinification is in large cement cuves, with very large old oak foudres as the alternative. The cooperative remains a significant force, although there has been the usual move towards estate bottling. When the wine was almost exclusively Grenache, it was never considered to have much aging potential—the usual advice was not to decant because it might oxidize in the decanter—but today there is more potential, although it remains true that most wines are best consumed within about five years.

The style is certainly softer than it used to be, but also significantly more refined. One major change in vinification has been the switch to destemming. "I think we are one of only three remaining estates that uses whole bunches," says Louis Barruol, who makes some of the most long-lived wines of the appellation at Château de Saint Cosme. "Before 1980 no one destemmed." Most Gigondas is aged in concrete cuves, but there is some use of wood, especially for special cuvées.

Gigondas has by far the greatest variation of terroir in the region. Vineyards extend from the surrounding plain, on to slopes near the village, and up the Dentelles approaching the summit. Extending from the village to the west, soils are rocky; on the Dentelles they are calcareous. It is quite a bit cooler on the Dentelles, and harvest can be as much as two weeks later. Soils are infertile, and yields are low.

How do you see the difference between Gigondas and Vacqueyras, I asked Jean-Michel Vache at Clos des Cazaux in Vacqueyras. "We are lucky because our Gigondas is high on the mountain and very stony, our Vacqueyras is more sandy. Because the terroirs are so very different, we don't have to create a difference," he says. I received a similar answer from Thierry Faravel at La Bouissière in Gigondas. "That's a difficult question, they are adjacent. It's easy for us because our Gigondas comes from the Dentelles, but on the plain there's only a stream separating the two. For us the Gigondas is finer, more mineral: the Vacqueyras is more rustic. For producers with vineyards in the plain, there is not much difference." As a practical matter, Vacqueyras is less well developed because most growers sell their grapes to the cooperative or to negociants; only a minority bottle their own wines.

The peak of the Dentelles is around 400m; the slope declines steeply past the village at 280m, then has a strong gradient going down to the main road at the west at around 200m, and declines more gradually to the western boundary of the appellation at around 120m. Taking the main road to define the boundary between the plateau to the west and the slopes to the east, probably around half of the vineyards are on the plateau (or garrigue as it is more euphemistically called in Gigondas), and half on the slopes, with half of the latter really well into the Dentelles on steeply terraced vineyards. "The three terroirs here are very different, but many people blend, so the discovery of terroir in the wines is limited. Harvest on the plateau is generally around 20-25 September, in the village at 30 September, and in the mountains around 10 October," says Louis Barruol.

The best wines of Gigondas tend to be special cuvées, often from old vines. These often come from near the village, as it was the first area to be planted. "I have been through years of experiments to find exceptional soils. The geologic diversity at Saint Cosme makes me

The Dentelles loom over vineyards on the plain below the village of Gigondas.

manage my estate like a Burgundy estate," says Louis Barruol. "I finished with three lieu-dits which have consistent and complex expression of the soil they come from. They are more or less old vines: from 50 to 130-years-old. Many lieu-dits were not interesting enough to be released."

A mainstream Gigondas, if we can use that term, can be robust, although it's likely to be smoother than it would have been a decade ago. By comparison, Châteauneuf-du-Pape has an extra sheen, another layer of sophistication. Gigondas solely from the plateau would be closer to Vacqueyras, with a more rustic impression. Yet Gigondas is really focused on Grenache, whereas Vacqueyras is turning to Syrah as an ameliorating influence.

"Gigondas typicity comes from the highest vineyards in the region plus the northwest exposure," says Yves Gras at Domaine Santa Duc. "In Vacqueyras they are developing Syrah, but Gigondas should focus on Grenache and Mourvèdre because they are at the northern limits." Syrah could well be a way forward (although at present the proportion is restricted by rules in both appellations). I tasted one wine in Vacqueyras where Syrah was the majority variety; albeit of dubious legality, this was the best wine I tasted from the appellation.

The problem of rising alcohol is exacerbated by the tendency of Grenache to build up sugar. "Grenache reaches phenolic maturity only at 14-14.5% in this region," says Cécile Dussere at Domaine de Mont-

The highest vineyards in Gigondas are terraced on the steep slopes of the Dentelles. This vineyard is at 350m altitude.

vac. "But appellation rules all over the southern Rhône require Grenache to be the dominant grape." Is the commitment to Grenache going to be a problem for Côtes du Rhône generally? "It *is* a problem, not it will be. It's getting close to a nightmare now. We have to get rid of Grenache, but the main trouble is that we are an AOP. Either we stay in the AOP and make undrinkable wine or we leave and make table wine," says Jean-Michel Vache. He is investigating some of the other varieties from Châteauneuf-du-Pape, and also increasing production of whites, especially Clairette, which is a low alcohol variety that still gives only around 13% in the present climate.

The plateau at the west of Gigondas extends south to Vacqueyras and north to Cairanne, which is the oldest of the named villages in the Côtes du Rhône, but curiously was one of the last to be promoted to appellation status. Why isn't Cairanne a Cru? I asked Laurent Brusset in Cairanne a few years ago. "It's a question of the people at the head of the appellation. In Gigondas there was a strong force with Gabriel Meffre. We had no one like that in Cairanne." In 2008 the producers started organizing to apply for promotion. "I think Cairanne will become a Cru because we have some young vignerons who are very motivated," Laurent said. Cairanne was finally promoted in 2015. My own sense is that with relatively homogeneous terroir, extending from garrigue to an alluvial plain, Cairanne is one of the best villages in the Côtes du Rhône.

Beaumes de Venise & Others

On the southeastern slopes of the Dentelles, only a dirt track separates Gigondas from Beaumes de Venise, but the appellations could scarcely be more different. Beaumes de Venise is known for vin doux naturel, a sweet, fortified, dessert-style wine made from Muscat. With its intensely grapey character, the wine has a distinctly perfumed quality that blends well with its sweet finish, but flavors tend to be straightforward rather than complex. There's also some dry Muscat made, but it must be labeled as IGP Vaucluse.

It's a sign of the times that red is more important in Beaumes de Venise than the traditional sweet Muscat. Top producer Domaine de Durban has always grown black grapes, but until recently sold them off or had them vinified elsewhere. Now they have a new cave specifically for producing red Beaumes de Venise. In the appellation as a whole, about two thirds of production is red, comprising GSM, and labeled with the appellation name since 2005. Beaumes de Venise is softer than Vacqueyras or Gigondas, and can be more immediately attractive, without having the overt fruitiness of the Côtes du Rhône.

Farther to the north, Rasteau was originally an AOP only for its sweet, fortified wine, in this case made as red, white, or rosé, mostly from Grenache (Noir or Blanc). But the quantity of fortified wine is very small (only 5% of total production). Since 2009, the AOP has also applied to dry red wine. Rasteau reds are a little harder than Beaumes de Venise when young, but quickly become soft and attractive. Like all the reds of the region, they are more refined than they used to be, and the best follow the style of Vacqueyras.

The other significant exception from red wine is Tavel, just north of Avignon on the west side of the river. Tavel produces only rosé, with Grenache and Cinsault as the main grapes. These are probably among the most powerful rosés of France, with a color that sometimes seems more like a light red wine.

Avignon forms the peak of a triangle, with the southern Rhône to its north, Provence to its east, and Languedoc to its west. Within thirty miles to the west is the old Roman city of Nîmes, center of the AOP Costières de Nîmes, a segue to the Languedoc. Costières de Nîmes became an AOC in the Languedoc region when it was promoted from VDQS in 1986, but in 1998 the producers requested that it should be attached to the Rhône wine region to reflect the true character of the wines. INAO approved the move to the Rhône in 2004.

Reference Wines for Southern Rhône Crus and Côtes

Gigondas	Domaine Les Pallières
	Château de Saint Cosme
Vacqueyras	Domaine le Clos des Cazaux
Rasteau (red)	Domaine de Beaurenard
Cairanne	Domaine Brusset
Sablet	Domaine Bertrand Stehelin
Séguret	Domaine de l'Amauve
Côtes du Rhône	Domaine Paul Autard
	Domaine Santa-Duc
Côtes du Rhône Villages	Château Sixtine
Lubéron	Château des Tourettes
Ventoux	La Martinelle
Costières de Nîmes	Château de la Tuilerie
Beaumes de Venise (VDN)	Domaine de Durban

So what is the typicity of Costières de Nîmes, I asked Chantale Comte at Château de la Tuilerie? "It's a good question, but I'm not sure there is a typicity," she says. "It's very variable. Anyway, it's not a feminine wine." There is more red wine than white, and there are complicated rules governing the blend. A combination of north-facing exposures, the effects of the mistral in winter, and the climatic influence of the sea in summer, reduces temperatures by 2-3 degrees, giving good acidity and enabling the whites to maintain freshness. The reds to my mind seem to be somewhat along the lines of Côtes du Rhône, at all events more resembling the rusticity of the south than the elegance of the northern Rhône.

Blending versus Cuvées

The tradition in the Rhône has always been for blending. The focus of the north on Syrah as its sole black variety meant that blending was directed towards combining lots from parcels with complementary terroirs. In the south, with less emphasis on terroir, blending focuses more on assemblage of different grape varieties. But in the past decade or so, there has been increasing emphasis on producing multiple cuvées. In the northern Rhône, they tend to represent single vineyards. In the south, cuvées tend to focus on selection, often of old vines, which pushes them towards more Grenache.

But the lack of any consistent focus creates potential for confusion. When a producer has multiple cuvées from a single appellation, each with a name intended to make it stand out from the crowd, the issue becomes how to resolve the significance of the name. Even in the Côtes du Rhône, most wines now have brand names; unless you are intimately familiar with the wines of the producer, it's impossible to know whether a name is a lieu-dit, an old vines selection, a special assemblage, or a brand name for some other selection. Even if it works for the producer, is it good for the region as a whole? Uncertainty is the enemy of sales.

Vintages

The first decade of the 2000s has shown extremes from the universal heat wave of 2003 to the floods of 2002 or high rainfall of 2008. The best recent vintage is 2016 or 2015, followed by 2010, and then 2005. The recent problem has been drought, marking vintages from 2015 on. The verdict is not yet in on how 2016 compares with 2015 overall. "It's incontestable that 2016 is better than 2015 in Châteauneuf-du-Pape," says Louis Barruol of Château Saint Cosme, "but it's difficult to say which is better in Gigondas."

2016	***	Producers consider this is a special year, with a good start to season with just enough rain, then dry conditions until mid September. Reds are intense and whites are elegant. Conventional wisdom is that wines get better going south, which places Châteauneuf-du-Pape at the top rating.
2015	***	A very ripe, large, vintage, making alcohol levels in the south even higher than usual.
2014		Difficulties in reaching ripeness for black grapes make this a year to approach cautiously in both north and south.
2013		The south was hit by a problem with flowering of Grenache, so reduced quantities mean wines are lighter in style (but more refreshing) than usual.

2012	**	Aside from intermittent rain, conditions were good in the south, much better than 2011, ripe but not over-ripe.
2011	*	A large vintage, more straightforward, emphasizing a fruity quality. Good but not comparable with 2010 or 2009.
2010	***	This is seen as the best vintage since 2005 because of its balance, ripeness and freshness. Aging potential is greater than usual.
2009	**	Vintage was a little too warm in some parts of the south and gave big wines with more tannins, classic in the sense of being robust and solid.
2008		Vintage was spoiled in both north and south by high rainfall in the summer. Some top cuvées were not produced.
2007	***	Wet Spring, but then high winds helped keep a generally fresh impression to this warm year, which is regarded as a top one in the south.
2006	*	A decent vintage but not considered as good in the south as in the north. Best wines have finesse but some are light.
2005	***	Considered the best year since 1990 in both north and south, giving wines with concentration and real longevity.
2004		Not many wines of interest today surviving in either north or south.
2003		Too hot everywhere: north better than south, but both questionable today.
2002		Poor all over southern France because of extensive floods.

Visiting the Region

The Southern Rhône is a large area, but the most interesting parts are Châteauneuf-du-Pape and the appellations around it—Gigondas, Vacqueyras, Beaumes de Venise, and some of the top villages of the Côtes du Rhône. Châteauneuf would be the obvious base in the immediate region, with many producers located in or close to the town. The major tourist attraction of Avignon is only about 20 minutes away,

Châteauneuf-du-Pape has an old town center with tiny streets that wind up to the ruined castle.

however, and it's perfectly feasible to stay there and go out to the vineyards for a day of visits.

Châteauneuf is the most tourist-oriented part of the region, and there are many tasting rooms open to visitors. Tasting rooms will usually be closed over the lunch break, from 12:00 to 2 p.m. As always, some producers do require appointments (especially smaller producers). Producers often have Côtes du Rhône to offer at tastings as well as red and white Châteauneuf-du-Pape, and (sometimes) special cuvées. A tasting usually lasts about an hour.

Some domains have an address that is only a zip code and a town name, sometimes with a lieu-dit added. Lieu-dits are mapped erratically, to say the least, in GPS devices in France, and the simplicity of the address does not necessarily mean the domain will be right in the center of town, however, as the zip code may extend well beyond into the countryside. Ask for directions and allow extra time.

Most producers now will sell wine directly to visitors. If you are presented with a price list at the end of the tasting, it is a sign that the producer will be disappointed if you leave without making a purchase.

The village square in Gigondas is at the end of a narrow street leading up from the plain below.

The etiquette of tasting assumes you will spit. A producer will be surprised if you drink the wine. Usually a tasting room or cellar is equipped with spittoons, but ask if you do not see one (crachoir in French). Of course, some tourists do enjoy drinking the wines, but producers will take you more seriously if you spit.

Châteauneuf-du-Pape has a smaller town center than you might expect from the fame of appellation, but it's very much oriented towards visitors interested in wine. The remnants of the castle loom above the town. Many producers are within easy reach. Gigondas is a very attractive little town, with some restaurants and cafes, just along from the Caveau de Gigondas, which offers free tastings for the wines of 75 producers. The village of Beaumes de Venise is a step down in interest.

Profiles of Leading Estates

Châteauneuf du Pape	*31*
Gigondas-Vacqueyras-Beaumes de Venise	*66*
Côtes du Rhône	*80*
Ventoux & Lubéron	*96*

Ratings

***	Excellent producers defining the very best of the appellation
**	Top producers whose wines typify the appellation
*	Very good producers making wines of character that rarely disappoint

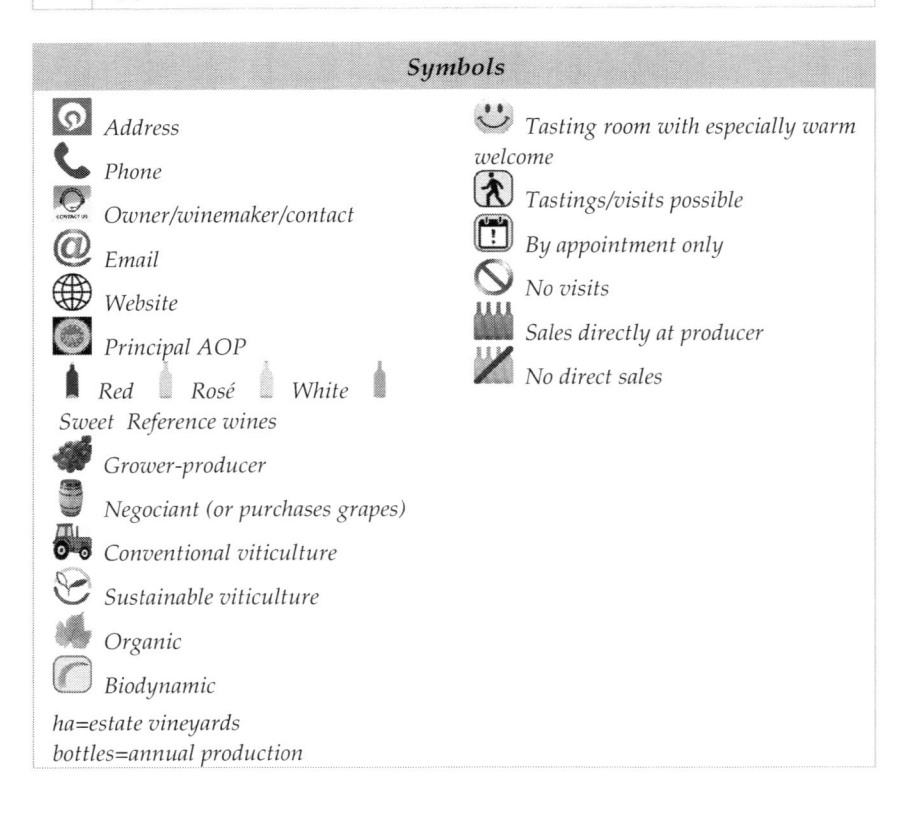

Symbols

- Address
- Phone
- Owner/winemaker/contact
- @ Email
- Website
- Principal AOP
- Red   Rosé   White
- Sweet Reference wines
- Grower-producer
- Negociant (or purchases grapes)
- Conventional viticulture
- Sustainable viticulture
- Organic
- Biodynamic

- Tasting room with especially warm welcome
- Tastings/visits possible
- By appointment only
- No visits
- Sales directly at producer
- No direct sales

ha=estate vineyards
bottles=annual production

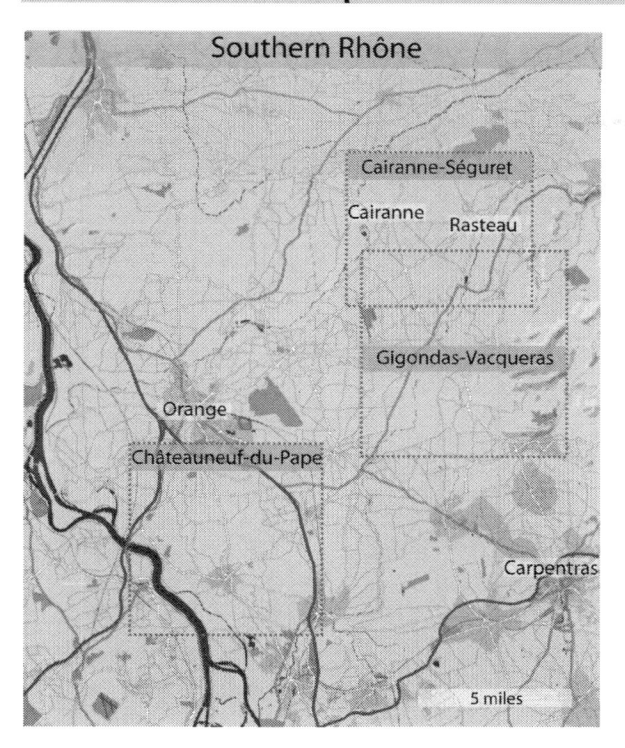

Châteauneuf du Pape

Southern Rhône

Cairanne-Séguret
Cairanne
Rasteau
Gigondas-Vacqueras
Orange
Châteauneuf-du-Pape
Carpentras

5 miles

Châteauneuf-du-Pape (AOP)

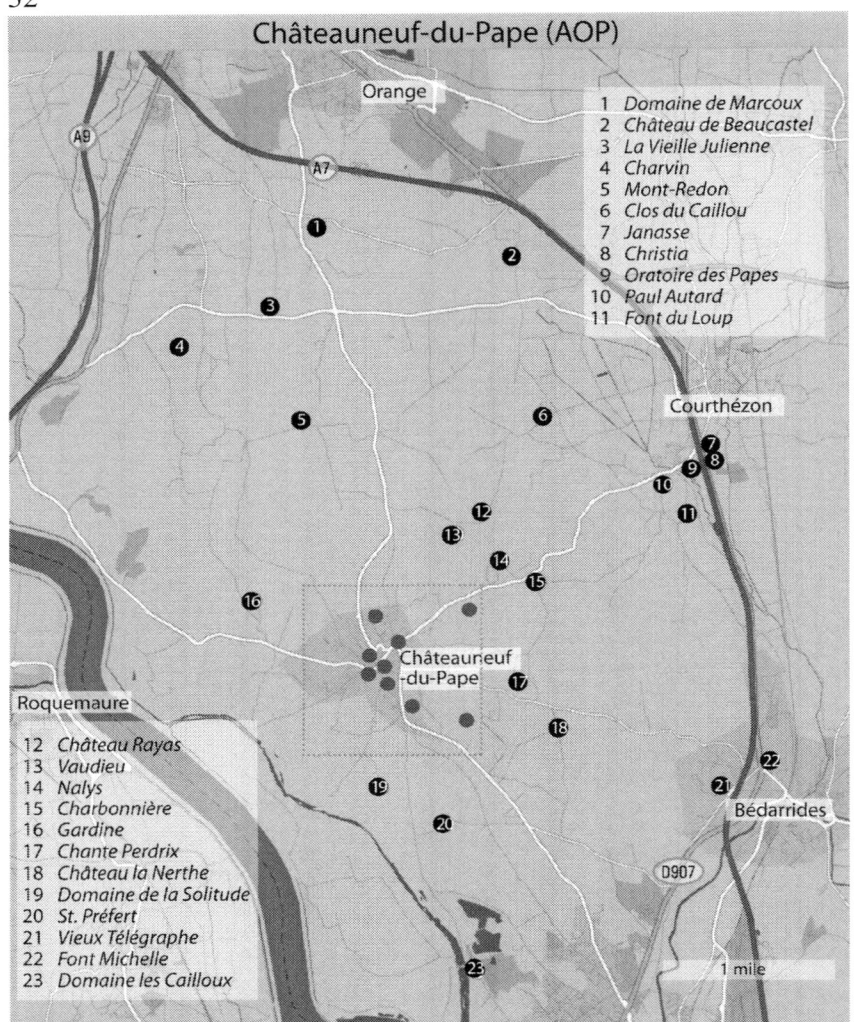

1. Domaine de Marcoux
2. Château de Beaucastel
3. La Vieille Julienne
4. Charvin
5. Mont-Redon
6. Clos du Caillou
7. Janasse
8. Christia
9. Oratoire des Papes
10. Paul Autard
11. Font du Loup
12. Château Rayas
13. Vaudieu
14. Nalys
15. Charbonnière
16. Gardine
17. Chante Perdrix
18. Château la Nerthe
19. Domaine de la Solitude
20. St. Préfert
21. Vieux Télégraphe
22. Font Michelle
23. Domaine les Cailloux

Châteauneuf-du-Pape (village)

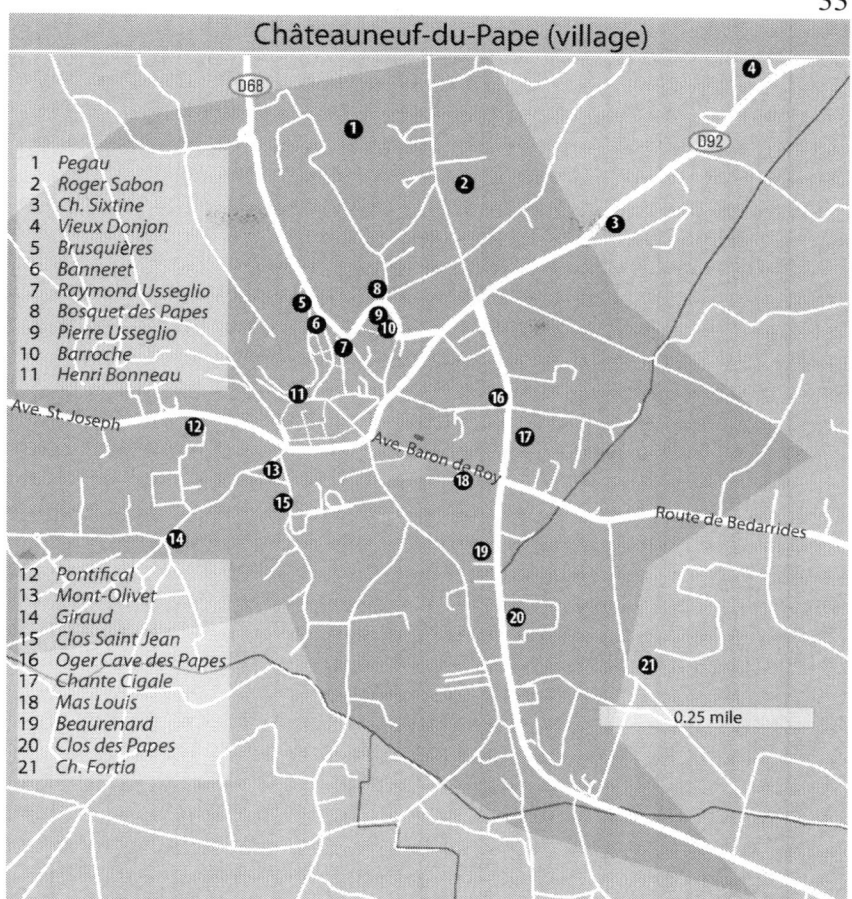

1. Pegau
2. Roger Sabon
3. Ch. Sixtine
4. Vieux Donjon
5. Brusquières
6. Banneret
7. Raymond Usseglio
8. Bosquet des Papes
9. Pierre Usseglio
10. Barroche
11. Henri Bonneau
12. Pontifical
13. Mont-Olivet
14. Giraud
15. Clos Saint Jean
16. Oger Cave des Papes
17. Chante Cigale
18. Mas Louis
19. Beaurenard
20. Clos des Papes
21. Ch. Fortia

Domaine Paul Autard **

Route de Châteauneuf-du-Pape, 84230 Courthézon

(33) 04 90 70 73 15

Jean-Paul & Pauline Autard

jean-paul.autard@wanadoo.fr

www.paulautard.com

Châteauneuf-du-Pape

Châteauneuf-du-Pape, La Côte Ronde

23 ha; 100,000 bottles

[map p. 32]

Located in the sandy area just at the northeastern edge of the Châteauneuf-du-Pape appellation, the domain has 10 ha within the AOP and another 13 ha just outside. Plantings are similar for both, with more than 70% Grenache, the rest being Syrah and Mourvèdre. The same elegant style runs through both the Châteauneuf-du-Pape and the Côtes du Rhône. Current winemaker Jean-Paul Autard, the fourth generation, who took over in 1997, thinks a lot of the elegance comes from destemming. "This allows us to do a lot of maceration because you're not obliged to stop because of extraction from the stems."

The Côtes du Rhône does not see wood, and is bottled in April following the vintage. The Châteauneuf-du-Pape has élevage in barriques, one third new. The cuvée La Côte Ronde uses 100% new oak for 17 months. Cuvée Juline offers a new twist: since 2008 it has been fermented in special barriques, made by Seguin Moreau, standing up with the top open; when fermentation is over, the missing end is put on, the barrel is put on its side, and élevage continues in the same barrique.

Jean-Paul is an arch modernist, but the style comes off, with unusual elegance for the Côtes du Rhône, refinement for the Châteauneuf-du-Pape, and a really modern, more oak-driven impression for the cuvées. Precision and purity of fruits are not descriptions that are usually at the forefront for Châteauneuf-du-Pape, but they are the most common terms found in my tasting notes here.

Château de Beaucastel   ***

739 Chemin Beaucastel, 84350 Courthézon
(33) 04 90 70 41 00
Kirsty Manahan
contact@beaucastel.com
www.beaucastel.com
Châteauneuf-du-Pape
Châteauneuf-du-Pape
94 ha; 300,000 bottles [map p. 32]

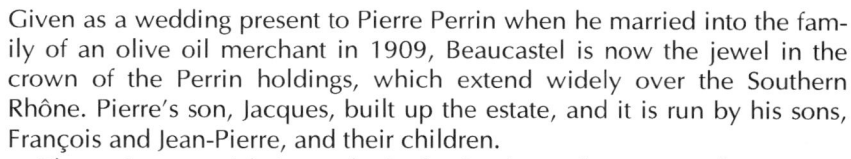

Given as a wedding present to Pierre Perrin when he married into the family of an olive oil merchant in 1909, Beaucastel is now the jewel in the crown of the Perrin holdings, which extend widely over the Southern Rhône. Pierre's son, Jacques, built up the estate, and it is run by his sons, François and Jean-Pierre, and their children.

The major part of their 330 ha in the Southern Rhône is Vieille Ferme, a vast enterprise making a million bottles per year of red and rosé Ventoux, and white Lubéron. The Côtes du Rhône (called Coudelet) comes partly from vineyards at the Beaucastel estate, just across the appellation boundary.

The vineyard occupies a vast, flat, stony area, with average vine age of 50-80 years. Château Beaucastel is well known for its commitment to maintain all the traditional grape varieties in Châteauneuf, but more to the point in terms of style is that the red is based on a high proportion of Mourvèdre (30%) with an equal proportion of Grenache (giving Beaucastel's wine the lowest proportion of Grenache in Châteauneuf). The special cuvée, Hommage à Jacques Perrin, has 60% Mourvèdre.

Red wine vinification uses a system of flash heating invented by Jacques Perrin. Unusually for Châteauneuf, the white is driven by Roussanne (80%), and there is also the famous Vieilles Vignes Roussanne bottling from a 2 ha plot of 90- to 100-year-old vines. .

Château Beaucastel was quite controversial through the 1980s and 1990s because of the presence of Brett in its wine (an earthy, leather note caused by the yeast Brettanomyces). They believe at Beaucastel that people may have confused Brett with the natural animal quality of Mourvèdre; but all the same, in the late nineties they renovated the cellars to eliminate Brett. Whether because of this cleanup or for other reasons I can't say, but I wasn't entirely sure I recognized the current vintages of Beaucastel when

I visited recently: they were far more overtly fruit-driven than the wines I remember from the last two decades of the twentieth century. Perhaps this is just the modern trend, but for whatever reason, the wines of today seem to have come more into the mainstream (meaning fruit-driven) of Châteauneuf-du-Pape. I find them technically better but less interesting, although maybe more to popular taste.

Domaine de Beaurenard ***

10 Avenue Pierre de Luxembourg, 84230 Châteauneuf-du-Pape
(33) 04 90 83 71 79
Paul Coulon
paul.coulon@beaurenard.fr
www.beaurenard.fr
Châteauneuf-du-Pape
Châteauneuf-du-Pape

66 ha; 250,000 bottles [map p. 33]

This is a family-owned domain, where Daniel Coulon and his brother represent the seventh generation. The 30 ha of vineyards in Châteauneuf-du-Pape are spread among more than 25 separate parcels, and there's an equal area of vineyards in Rasteau and the Côtes du Rhône. The Coulons are committed to biodynamic viticulture, and because the vineyard holdings are so broken up, they have to be quite forceful sometimes to stop treatments from their neighbors from encroaching. They are committed to maintaining all thirteen varieties and do their own selection and grafting. Fermentation occurs in stainless steel or wood, and the wine matures in foudres (with the only break from tradition being the use of a small proportion of barriques). Bottling is done by the phases of the moon.

In both Rasteau and Châteauneuf there is a regular bottling and special cuvée. The Rasteau is quite appealing, and the special cuvée, called Les Argiles Bleues after a 2 ha plot of clay terroir, is more sophisticated. The red Châteauneuf, based on 70% Grenache, has good structure when young, but quickly becomes more supple. The real mark of elegance comes with the Boisrenard special cuvée (not made every year), from vines planted in 1902; the red is elegant (based on 60% Grenache), and the white is quite unctuous, showing its barrel-fermentation and maturation in oak. There used to be 10 ha for Boisrenard, but the need to replant has reduced the plot to 6 ha.

Domaine Henri Bonneau ***

Châteauneuf-du-Pape
APPELLATION CHATEAUNEUF - DU - PAPE CONTROLEE

Réserve des / Célestins

Product of France / Red Rhone Wine
Alc. 14 % vol. / 750 ml

HENRI BONNEAU VIGNERON CHATEAUNEUF-DU-PAPE (VAUCLUSE) FRANCE

35 Rue Ducos, 84230 Châteauneuf-du-Pape

(33) 04 90 83 73 08

Daniel Combin

@ distribution.danielcombin@orange.fr

Châteauneuf-du-Pape

Châteauneuf-du-Pape, Marie Beurrier

10 ha; 16,000 bottles

[map p. 33]

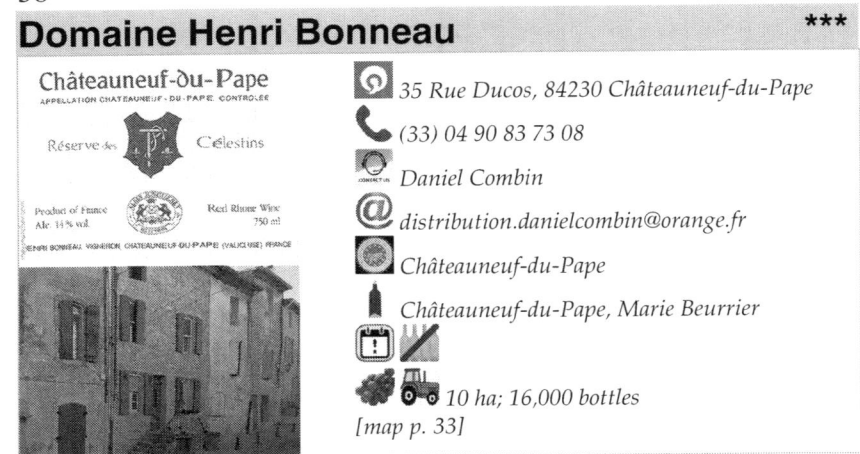

Henri Bonneau was a living legend in Châteauneuf. It was all but impossible to arrange a visit to the old cellars, filled with decrepit-looking barrels, located in the center of the town (with a permanent hand-written sign saying "cave fermé"). The vineyards are broken up into many plots. This is the quintessential Grenache-driven domain, but one note of distinction is that the vines are (relatively) young, between 30 and 50 years old: Henri did not like very old vines, and believed that the useful life span is fifty years. Typically there is not much detailed information about breakdown of grape varieties, but Grenache is probably more than 90%, with the rest consisting of Mourvèdre, Counoise, and Vaccarèse.

Henri was famous for picking late and achieving super-ripeness. Winemaking was famously traditional, with fermentation in concrete cuves followed by maturation in old barriques. In addition to the regular cuvée, the Cuvée Marie Beurrier and Cuvée des Célestins were produced when vintage conditions were deemed appropriate. The decision was taken only at the time of bottling, several years after the vintage. This must surely have been the longest élevage in the appellation. Bonneau distinguished his three cuvées as "good, very good, and grand vin." With Jacques Reynaud no longer on the scene at Château Rayas, Henri Bonneau was by far the most idiosyncratic producer in Châteauneuf-du-Pape until his death in 2016, leaving the future of the domain uncertain, but his family are continuing to run it.

Domaine Les Cailloux

2648, chemin de l'Ile de l'Oiselay, 84700 Sorgues

(33) 04 90 83 72 62

Fabrice Brunel

fabrice.brunel@domaine-les-cailloux.fr

domaine-les-cailloux.fr

Châteauneuf-du-Pape

Châteauneuf-du-Pape

60 ha; 400,000 bottles

[map p. 32]

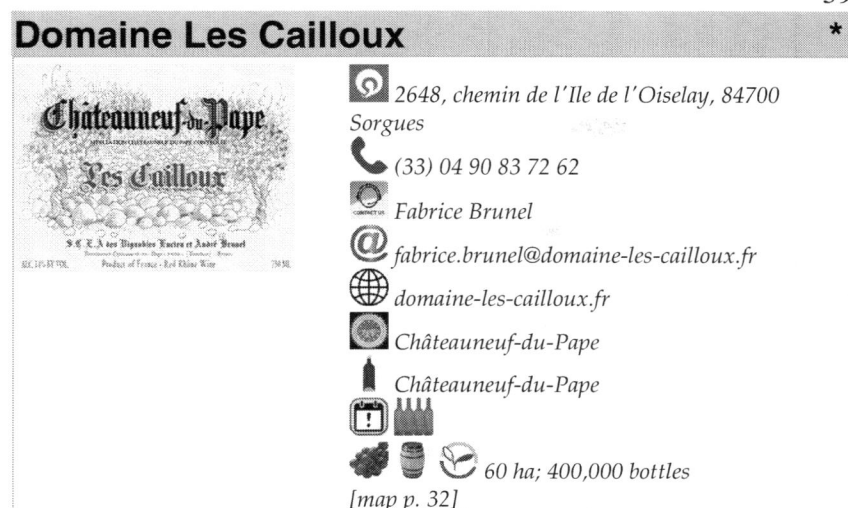

Disentangling the different wines made by André Brunel can be confusing. There's a Côtes du Rhône under the label Domaine André Brunel. There's another from Domaine de la Becassonne, a small estate just to the east of the Châteauneuf-du-Pape AOP, which makes exclusively white wine. The Brunel business is 40% negociant and 60% from estate holdings in the Côtes du Rhône (11 ha) and Châteauneuf-du-Pape (22 ha). "We are a classical family of Châteauneuf-du-Pape, we have had wines in our family for 300 years," says Fabrice Brunel.

The jewel of the holdings is the Châteauneuf-du-Pape, Domaine Les Cailloux, whose Le Centenaire was one of the first special cuvées, with only 300 cases from an 0.80 ha parcel. Les Cailloux's nominal address is in the town of Châteauneuf-du-Pape, but I went to a utilitarian warehouse on the outskirts in Sorgues to meet Fabrice, who has come into the business to take over the commercial side and let his father concentrate on what he likes best—"he's happiest driving his tractor through the vineyards," Fabrice says.

The Châteauneuf is fairly full bodied and shows its dominant Grenache component in the old tradition of the appellation. Le Centenaire originated as a special cuvée to celebrate the hundredth anniversary of the vineyard. "Since then, the wine from Centenaire has always been vinified separately, and at assemblage we decide whether to bottle it separately or include it in the general Châteauneuf," Fabrice explains.

Domaine Chante Cigale *

7 Avenue Louis Pasteur, 84230 Châteauneuf-du-Pape

(33) 04 90 83 70 57

Christian Favier

info@chante-cigale.com

www.chante-cigale.com

Châteauneuf-du-Pape

47 ha; 160,000 bottles

[map p. 33]

One of the larger family domains in the appellation, Chante Cigale has operated more or less under its present name since it was called Clos Chante Cigale in 1874. Alexandre Favier took over the domain in 2002, straight from oenology school. Vineyards are mostly in Châteauneuf-du-Pape (40 ha), with more than forty parcels dispersed around the appellation, including all the types of terroir, and there are also cuvées from the Côtes du Rhône and IGP Méditerranée.

The domain is one of the largest producers of white Châteauneuf-du-Pape, which is about 20% of production. The regular cuvée is quite powerful and aromatic, but the fruits are cut by a touch of salinity. Perhaps this is due to the recent inclusion of 20% Picpoul (a grape known for its high acidity), from vines planted a few years ago. The Extrait while is 80% Roussanne and 20% Clairette; "we tried 100% Roussanne," says winemaker Jean-Yves Pomaret, "but it was too fat, so we are blending the Roussanne with some Clairette." Very fine and silky, it too has a touch of salinity.

The red Tradition Châteauneuf is 65% Grenache, 20% Syrah, 10% Mourvèdre, and ages 70% in cuve. It tends towards a relatively fresh style. The Vieilles Vignes is a GSM from four plots of old vines, with a similar aging regime, and is more concentrated but has a touch of minerality to counterpoise the fruits. It ages well. Made in very small amounts, Extrait is unusual blend of a majority (70-80%) of Mourvèdre with a minority of Grenache, from 100-year-old vines in a single vineyard, aged in demi-muids. Spice and dense, it is strongly structured—Jean-Yves compares it to Bandol—and is a true vin de garde.

Domaine Chante Perdrix

Vignoble Nicolet, 501 Chemin du Plan du Rhône, 84230 Châteauneuf-du-Pape

(33) 04 90 83 71 86

Frédéric & Franck Nicolet

contact@chante-perdrix.com

www.chante-perdrix.com

Châteauneuf-du-Pape

20 ha; 40,000 bottles
[map p. 32]

The domain was established in 1896 in the southern part of the appellation, where its vineyards are on the famous galets. It expanded when the vineyards of Domaine Perges came into the family by inheritance. It is now managed by the fourth and fifth generations, Frédéric et Franck Nicolet. All the vineyards are in Châteauneuf-du-Pape, almost in one block, planted with black varieties, except for 0.5 ha of white. There was a single red and white until 2015, but this was an exceptional year, and Frédéric's son Franck was the driving force for introducing special cuvées of monovarietals.

The white Châteauneuf is half Clairette (aged in wood) and half Grenache (aged in stainless steel). It's slightly aromatic and fresh. The Etienne Pecoul cuvée (named for the founder of the domain) is 100% Clairette, vinified and aged in new demi-muids. It's more powerful, with a greater sense of fat to the palate. There is no malolactic fermentation for the whites.

The red is a GSM blend with 60% Grenache (aged in foudres), 20% Syrah (aged in barriques), and 15% Mourvèdre, and small amounts of other varieties. It shows its structure when young; Frédéric thinks it is usually ready after 3-4 years. Etienne Pecoul is 100% Grenache, aged in new demi-muids. Deep and black, it shows the aromatics of Grenache, with its structure hidden underneath. Henri Perges is 100% Mourvèdre, also aged in new demi-muids; rather tight on release, it is spicy and taut.

Domaine Clos du Caillou *

1600, Chemin Saint-Dominique, 84350 Courthézon

(33) 04 90 70 73 05

Bruno Gaspard

closducaillou@wanadoo.fr

www.closducaillou.com

Châteauneuf-du-Pape

Châteauneuf-du-Pape, Les Safres

53 ha; 180,000 bottles

[map p. 32]

Located at Courthézon at the northeast boundary of Châteauneuf, Clos du Caillou is an oddity: it's virtually an enclave surrounded by Châteauneuf vineyards, but only 8 ha of the domain are classified in the AOP, the rest being Côtes du Rhône. The reason lies in the history of the domain: when Châteauneuf was classified in 1936, the owner of the time refused admission to the authorities, so the vineyards were not classified, although they almost certainly otherwise would have been included in Châteauneuf. The present ownership dates from 1956, with additional vineyards planted in 1995.

Black grape plantings are 80% Grenache. The main cuvée was known originally simply as Clos du Caillou but now is called Les Safres: this is 95% Grenache and aged conventionally in old foudres. Les Quartz comes from old vines Grenache (85%) and Syrah, sourced from two specific vineyard parcels. It's aged in a mixture of tronconique cuves and foudres. The top cuvée, La Réserve, has 60% Grenache, 20% Mourvèdre, and 20% Syrah, and is matured in a mixture of concrete vats and new and old demi-muids.

There's a matching range of Côtes du Rhône: the main cuvée is called Le Bouquet des Garrigues; Le Clos du Caillou comes from the most interior parcels; Les Quartz comes from parcels very close to those used for the old vines Grenache in the Châteauneuf Les Quartz; and La Réserve is a selection of the best lots. There are also whites from both Châteauneuf and Côtes du Rhône.

Château de la Font du Loup *

Route de Châteauneuf, 84350 Courthézon
(33) 04 90 33 06 34
Anne-Charlotte Mélia-Bachas
contact@lafontduloup.com
www.melia.fr
Châteauneuf-du-Pape

20 ha; 50,000 bottles
[map p. 32]

"This place is different," says Anne-Charlotte Mélia-Bachas. Indeed it is. Font du Loup is at the eastern border of Châteauneuf-du-Pape, with a single block of north-facing vineyards from which you can see across to Mont Ventoux. "It's always windy here, and the soils are sandy. This means we cannot make super-extracted and powerful wines," she says. "We expect our terroir to give us freshness and delicacy." The cool wind from Mont Ventoux makes for a cool, fresh, microclimate.

The domain is at the end of a very long track that winds for a couple of miles from its official address on the main road from Châteauneuf to Courthézon, and occupies one of the highest points of the appellation, on the edge of the plateau of Crau. The name means Fountain of the Wolf, from a legend that wolves stopped here on their way south from Mont Ventoux. "My great grandfather bought the property almost 100 years ago. We have the same vineyards now except for a parcel of 4 ha added in 2012." Vineyards are all around the cellar; the average age of the vines is 65 years. Because the vineyards are north-facing, harvest is about two weeks later than the rest of the appellation. Plantings are the usual GSM trio—there is only just over a hectare of white varieties—with Grenache and Mourvèdre the most successful varieties. In addition to Châteauneuf-du-Pape, there are 7 ha of vineyards rented in the Côtes du Rhône.

The Melia family bought this property in 1942. Anne Charlotte and her husband Laurent Bachas (the winemaker) took over in 2002 after her father left for Morocco to start a new venture. The major cuvée is Tradition, 65% Grenache, 20% Syrah, 10% Mourvèdre, and 5% Cinsault, with Grenache and Cinsault aged in foudres, and Syrah and Mourvèdre in 2-year barriques and demi-muids. Le Puy Rolland comes from a single parcel of old vines Grenache. There's also a Côtes du Rhône from Syrah and Grenache. The white Châteauneuf is a blend of several varieties, aged in a mix of barriques and demi-muids.

Château Fortia *

10 Route de Bédarrides, 84231 Châteauneuf-du-Pape

(33) 04 90 83 72 25

Pierre Pastre or Anna Olejnik

chateaufortia@gmail.com

www.chateau-fortia.com

Châteauneuf-du-Pape

Château Fortia

Châteauneuf-du-Pape

32 ha; 125,000 bottles

[map p. 33]

One of the oldest producers in Châteauneuf-du-Pape, Château Fortia was making wine in the mid eighteenth century. By the twentieth century, it was owned by Baron Roy de Boiseaumarié, who was instrumental in establishing the appellation system in France, and responsible for Châteauneuf-du-Pape becoming one of the first AOCs. Just southeast of the town, the domain remains in the hands of the Boiseaumarié family. The building is a genuine château, dating from the nineteenth century (some of the cellars date from the fourteenth century). The vineyards are in a single block around the château.

The traditional red Châteauneuf is 80% Grenache to 20% Syrah; the special cuvée, La Cuvée du Baron, reduces the Grenache to 50%, with 45% Syrah and 5% Mourvèdre. The latest innovation, unusual for the region, almost reverses the proportions of the traditional cuvée, and really focuses on Syrah; the Cuvée Réserve has 85% Syrah and 15% Mourvèdre. Winemaker Pierre Pastre says, "We found some old bottles in the cellar, they were remarkable, and my father-in-law finally remembered he had done an experiment with pure Syrah one year. So I have made a cuvée of Syrah with Mourvèdre, because I think Grenache doesn't do well with Syrah." There is also a white, in which malolactic fermentation is blocked to retain freshness. Aside from the new cuvée, the approach is traditional, and aging for all wines is exclusively in foudres.

Château de la Gardine ★★

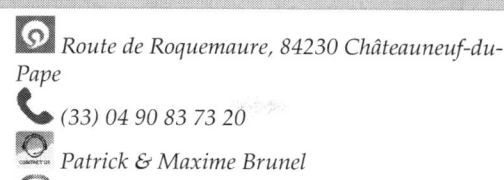

Route de Roquemaure, 84230 Châteauneuf-du-Pape
(33) 04 90 83 73 20
Patrick & Maxime Brunel
gardine.export@gardine.com
www.gardine.com
Châteauneuf-du-Pape

54 ha; 210,000 bottles
[map p. 32]

On the western edge of the appellation, La Gardine is unusual in having its vineyards in a single large parcel. Before the Revolution, it was a large farm owned by the Bishop of Avignon. The estate was purchased in 1945 by Gaston Brunel (a well known negociant), when it was in poor shape with only 10 ha of vines. Gaston enlarged the vineyards by planting new plots on the garrigue. Today there are 20 ha of woods remaining.

In 1963 the Brunels expanded by buying vineyards in Rasteau, where the 52 ha estate has 40 ha classified as Rasteau and 12 ha in Côtes du Rhône. In 1998 they purchased Château Saint Roch (see mini-profile) in Roquemaure (with 40 ha facing La Gardine across the Rhône). Ten years ago, they also started a negociant activity, Brunel Père & Fils, which makes wine from the Côtes du Rhône and the Crus of the north. Production from the negociant is a bit larger than from the estate. The Brunels are considered to be modernists across the range, with quite a bit of new oak used for the top appellations.

The difference between the reds from Rasteau and the adjacent vineyard in Côtes du Rhône Village (just a little lower down) is slight. Both are three quarters Grenache to one quarter Syrah, fermented in concrete, and show the same approachable, rich style. While the Village wine really shows Grenache, the sense of structure from Syrah is just a touch more evident in the Rasteau.

For white wines at Châteauneuf, "We are very strong on Roussanne," says marketing manager Alban de Gérin. "It's very important for us to avoid something fat. We never do MLF." The white is a third Roussanne fermented and aged in new barriques, combined with other varieties fermented in stainless steel. The top cuvée is Marie Léoncie, 90% old vines Roussanne and 10% Clairette, whole cluster-fermented in new oak. Spicy oak hides the stone fruits of peaches when it is released, then the palate deepens and becomes steadily more honeyed over the next 10-15 years.

The estate red Châteauneuf is a classic GSM blend with small amounts of other varieties, aged in a mix of concrete and 2-year barriques. It ages well, although after a decade the underlying structure becomes a bit more apparent. Gaston Philippe is a third each of old vines Grenache, Mourvèdre, and Syrah, from the best plots — not necessarily the oldest — aged in new barriques. As it ages, that plush edge is replaced by more complex flavor variety, and it reaches its peak after about 15 years. L'Immortelle comes from sorting out the ripest grapes from the parcels that are used for Gaston Philippe. It's richer, and as it ages, shows more the impression of old vines Grenache. The general style brings out the fruits, but with good supporting structure for aging, and tends, if not to vin de garde, at least to wine that repays aging.

Domaine de La Janasse *

DOMAINE DE LA JANASSE
Vieilles Vignes

CHÂTEAUNEUF DU PAPE
2007

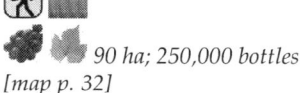

27, Chemin du Moulin, 84350 Courthézon
(33) 04 90 70 86 29
Christophe Sabon
lajanasse@gmail.com
www.lajanasse.com
Châteauneuf-du-Pape
Châteauneuf-du-Pape, Tradition

90 ha; 250,000 bottles
[map p. 32]

The domain is located in Courthézon, on the other side of the autoroute from Châteauneuf-du-Pape, but has more than fifty separate vineyard parcels scattered around the eastern part of the appellation, mostly on gravelly-sandy soils. Founded in 1967, grapes were originally sold to the cooperative, but Aimé Sabon built a cellar and started domain-bottling in 1973; since 1991 the domain has been run by his children Christophe and Isabelle. There are 20 ha in Châteauneuf-du-Pape, with other holdings in Côtes du Rhône, just to the north of Châteauneuf.

The Tradition cuvée consists of 80% Grenache, 10% Syrah, and 10% Mourvèdre; Cuvée Chaupin comes exclusively from Grenache planted in 1912 on sandy soils in the northern part of the appellation a (slightly cooler location); and the Vieilles Vignes cuvée is a blend based on 85% Grenache, from vines that are 100-years old. Tradition plays more to elegance than power, Chaupin is atypical for old vines Grenache in showing more freshness than usual, and the Vieilles Vignes really gives the impression of being dominated by very old Grenache.

Oak is not obtrusive in any of the cuvées. Wines are matured in a mixture of (mostly) foudres and barriques or demi-muids, with only a little new oak. The style here is dominated by Grenache. His American importer describes Christophe as a "self-proclaimed defender of Grenache."

The regular white cuvée is a blend of Grenache Blanc, Clairette, and Roussanne, but the white Cuvée Prestige comes from old vines, 60% of which are Roussanne. Unusually for the region, the whites go through malolactic fermentation. The Côtes du Rhônes are relatively light, intended for current consumption.

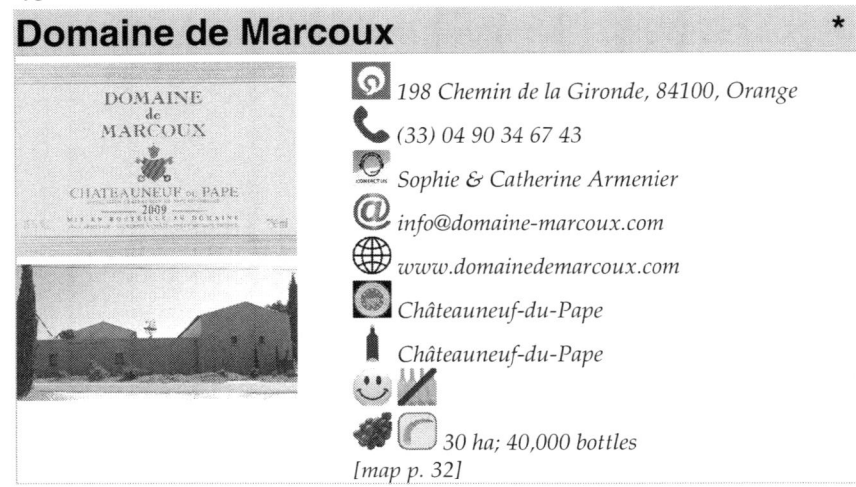

Domaine de Marcoux *

198 Chemin de la Gironde, 84100, Orange
(33) 04 90 34 67 43
Sophie & Catherine Armenier
info@domaine-marcoux.com
www.domainedemarcoux.com
Châteauneuf-du-Pape
Châteauneuf-du-Pape

30 ha; 40,000 bottles
[map p. 32]

Sisters Sophie and Catherine Armenier have run this domain since 1993; Sophie handles vinification and Catherine manages the vineyard. In addition to 19 ha in Châteauneuf, they have some Côtes du Rhône and also some plots for Vin de France, both near the winery but across the appellation boundary, and an 8 ha domain in Lirac, which they purchased in 2010. They would like to buy more Côtes du Rhône; in fact they found the vineyard in Lirac when looking for Côtes du Rhône.

The winery is at the north of Châteauneuf-du-Pape (actually quite close to Orange) but the vineyards are mostly in the south, although with some in the east at La Crau, and in the west, so terroirs range from galets to sandy to calcareous. Each area is vinified separately. Everything is completely destemmed, and only pumping-over is used for extraction; some barriques are used for Syrah and Mourvèdre but most élevage is in cuve.

The style here is quite fine, but distinctly rich, with alcohol often pushing up well over 15%. I like the purity of the fruits, but find a slightly sweet touch to the finish (most likely derived from the high alcohol), sometimes to be a little disconcerting. The Vieilles Vignes is always distinctly more forceful than the regular bottling, partly due to extra concentration from the old vines, and partly because the proportion of Grenache is higher. The wines take five or six years to come into their own, and by a decade usually begin to show some tertiary complexity.

Clos du Mont-Olivet *

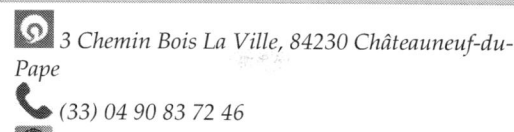

3 Chemin Bois La Ville, 84230 Châteauneuf-du-Pape

(33) 04 90 83 72 46

Jean-Claude, Pierre & Bernard Sabon

contact@clos-montolivet.fr

www.clos-montolivet.com

Châteauneuf-du-Pape

Châteauneuf-du-Pape

47 ha; 200,000 bottles
[map p. 33]

Mont Olivet is owned by a branch of the Sabons, an old Châteauneuf winemaking family. This domain was founded by Séraphin Sabon in 1932; it later became one of the first estates to bottle its own wine, and is run by the fourth generation today. (In the early 1950s, the vineyards that are now part of Roger Sabon were split off.)

There are 28 ha of vineyards spread throughout the Châteauneuf appellation in many small holdings, with further vineyards about twenty miles to the north in the Côtes du Rhône. In Châteauneuf, the domain is driven by Grenache, whereas in the Côtes du Rhône, plantings are divided more or less equally between Grenache and Syrah. The traditional Châteauneuf has 80% Grenache. Le Petit Mont is effectively a second wine, produced from young vines, and is 95% Grenache. (Does this imply an even more Grenache-driven future at Mont Olivet?) A special cuvée, the Cuvée de Papet, is produced in some vintages from 80- to 100-year-old vines in the walled vineyard of Montolivet in the eastern part of the appellation, and the grape mix here has varied from 75% to 95% Grenache.

Winemaking is traditional, with only partial destemming, and all cuvées matured in neutral foudres. The single white is fairly mainstream, although sometimes I find it to lack character (admittedly this is a criticism I have of many white Châteauneufs.). The style of the reds is sturdy and ageworthy, not overdone, although the Cuvée de Papet is more exotic.

Château Mont-Redon *

Chemin de Maucoil, 84231 Châteauneuf-du-Pape

(33) 04 90 83 72 75

Pierre Fabre

contact@chateaumontredon.fr

www.chateaumontredon.fr

Châteauneuf-du-Pape

100 ha; 500,000 bottles
[map p. 32]

This domain has a very old name, but dates effectively from 1923, when Henri Plantin bought a property of 186 ha with 2.5 ha of vineyards. "No one wanted the property because it was so far out. There were 186 ha and over the generations, we've planted more vineyards," says his great grandson Pierre Fabre, who took over in 2017 when his father and uncle retired. "We've gone from 2 ha to 100 ha, and we've only bought 1 ha in that period." Mont-Redon still feels a bit out of the way today; leaving the village of Châteauneuf, you go through a narrow forested road before coming back out into the vineyards of the Cabrières plateau. The winery itself is fairly well set off from the road, entirely surrounded by vineyards. Situated in the northwest quadrant, the vineyards are in one block on the highest point of the appellation, with varied soils.

Mont-Redon has expanded into other areas, in the 1981s purchasing the 20 ha Château de Sablet in the Côtes du Rhône (near Roquemaure on the other side of the Rhône), in 1997 a domain with 33 ha in Lirac, and most recently the Château Riotor with 40 ha in the Côtes de Provence. There's also a negociant activity for producing Côtes du Rhône. There's roughly an equal amount of production from the domain and from the negociant.

"Fermentation here is all about stainless steel," Pierre says, as he shows you round the vast tank room in the new winery that was built into the hillside in 2010. The red Châteauneuf ages half in tank and half in oak, but good vintages get more oak. Since 2011 selection has been stricter and stricter. The best lots go into Châteauneuf du Pape, but other lots are declassified and sold off as bulk wine. Up to 2018 there has been only one cuvée in white and one red, but that is changing. "We are introducing special cuvees in top vintages, but only 1-2% of production because I wouldn't want the main cuvee to be reduced in quality."

The whites are light and attractive, from Côtes du Rhône through Lirac to Châteauneuf, intended for immediate enjoyment. The reds go from the light, fresh fruits of Côtes du Rhône (80% Grenache with 20% Syrah), the greater density but still pure style of the Lirac GSM blend, to the more structured impression of Châteauneuf-du-Pape, where Pierre says of the current vintage, "This is drinkable now, but it is absolutely not ready, it should be left in the cellar for about five years easy." The clean purity of the house style may be partly explained by viticultural policy: "We are the earliest pickers in the Rhône valley. I believe in the power of acidity to support long-term aging. Mont-Redon is known for its ability to age."

Château La Nerthe **

Route de Sorgues, 84230 Châteauneuf-du-Pape
(33) 04 90 83 70 11
Ralph Garcin
visit@chateaulanerthe.fr
www.chateaulanerthe.fr
Châteauneuf-du-Pape
Châteauneuf-du-Pape, Cuvée des Cadettes
92 ha; 300,000 bottles
[map p. 32]

The history of La Nerthe goes way back to when it was known as La Ferme de Bourguignon. In the sixteenth century it began to be known as La Nerthe. By the seventeenth century there were 25 ha of vineyards. "At this time, Châteauneuf-du-Pape was not known, but La Nerthe was already known; by the end of the nineteenth century people were talking about the quality of La Nerthe," says winemaker Christian Voeux, who came here from Château Mont Redon in 2008. Current ownership dates from 1985.

This is a large domain, extended by a 21 ha purchase in 1991, with an unusually high proportion (15%) of white wine. Surrounded by galets, the Château sits on the western edge of the famous La Crau plateau; vineyards are in two large blocks. The special cuvée, Cuvée des Cadettes, is made only in some years by a selection from the best old vines of the Château (around 100 years old); it is a blend of Grenache, Syrah, and Mourvèdre like the main cuvée of La Nerthe. The style is relatively restrained, usually with around 55% Grenache in La Nerthe, and a little less in Cuvée des Cadettes. There's also a cuvée from young vines (young in this context means less than 20 years), the Clos de la Granière. In addition to the white La Nerthe, there is also the cuvée Clos de Beauvenir, which carries more obvious wood. The mark of the house style is freshness. "I always look for freshness and natural acidity to safeguard the fruit," Christian says. The wines achieve more subtlety than is common in Châteauneuf. The style of the winemaker shows through also at his family estate, Domaine de l'Amauve (see mini-profile), where he also makes the wines.

Clos des Papes ★★

13, Avenue Pierre de Luxembourg, 84230 Châteauneuf-du-Pape

(33) 04 90 83 70 13

Paul-Vincent Avril

clos-des-papes@clos-des-papes.com

www.clos-des-papes.fr

Châteauneuf-du-Pape

Châteauneuf-du-Pape

37 ha; 60,000 bottles   [map p. 33]

Clos des Papes is one of the classic estates of Châteauneuf-du-Pape, founded by Paul Avril who began producing wine in 1896 and was subsequently involved in the creation of the appellation (but the Avril's history in the town goes back further, as noted on the label, as the Avrils were involved in the politics of Châteauneuf from 1756 to 1790).

Vineyards are concentrated around the town of Châteauneuf-du-Pape, but the 24 different parcels extend throughout the appellation (including 7 ha on the plateau of Le Crau); 4 ha in the cooler areas are used for the white wine, and the rest are used for the red blend. Most of the vines are more than 50-years-old. (The domain takes its name from a plot close to the ruined castle in the town, which was originally a clos that was a papal vineyard.) There are 5 ha outside the appellation, which are used to make a Vin de France, Le Petit Vin d'Avril (both red and white, usually a blend across vintages).

Clos des Papes is a traditional domain in the sense of producing only one cuvée of red and one of white, a policy established by Paul Avril, who ran the estate from 1963 to 1987, and believed in "one estate, one wine." Yields are kept low, less than 28 hl/ha. Grenache is only about two thirds of the blend, with a high proportion of Mourvèdre (20%); the rest is essentially Syrah with very small amounts of Vaccarèse, Counoise and Muscardin. The white is a more or less equal blend of five varieties (Clairette, Bourboulenc, Grenache Blanc, Roussanne and Picpoul).

The domain has been run by Vincent Avril since 1987. Style is partly determined by Vincent's five years at school in Burgundy, which gave him a taste for moderation. Vincent introduced destemming, for example. He's been known to say, "I take it as a compliment when people tell me that Clos des Papes makes a wine almost in the style of a Burgundy!"

Domaine du Pegau *

15 Avenue Impérial, 84230 Châteauneuf-du-Pape

(33) 04 90 83 72 70

Laurence Feraud

pegau@pegau.com

www.pegau.com

Châteauneuf-du-Pape

Châteauneuf-du-Pape, Réservée

23 ha; 80,000 bottles

[map p. 33]

This is a relatively recent domain, created by Paul Féraud (a school friend of Henri Bonneau) and his daughter Laurence in 1987 (although the estate has existed under the name of Domaine Féraud since the eighteenth century). Initially there were only 7 ha. There are 21 ha of plantings in 11 separate vineyard parcels throughout the Châteauneuf appellation; in 2012 the Férauds purchased another estate at Sorgues, just to the south of the appellation, now known as Château Pegau, which has 25 ha in the Côtes du Rhône Villages, 5 ha in Côtes du Rhône, and another 11 ha used for Vin de France. There are also negociant wines under the Féraud name.

Vinification of the Châteauneuf-du-Pape is quite traditional with no destemming. There are several cuvées: all the reds are 70% or 80% Grenache. The regular cuvée is called Réservée and spends 18 months in foudres; there is also a white. There are two special red cuvées. The Cuvée da Capo, made most years, comes from a plot on La Crau and follows the same regime as the regular bottling, but is a selection of the best lots (usually one foudre). The Cuvée Laurence is also based on selection, but the wine matures much longer, for 36 months in foudres or old barriques, depending on the vintage: it is intended to be a long-lived, traditional style. Alcohol is high, and the style is lush and robust. Domaine du Pegau is widely considered to be a standard bearer for the traditional style of Châteauneuf-du-Pape. In addition to the appellation, the domain has 20 ha of vineyards for producing Vin de France rosé and red.

Château Rayas ***

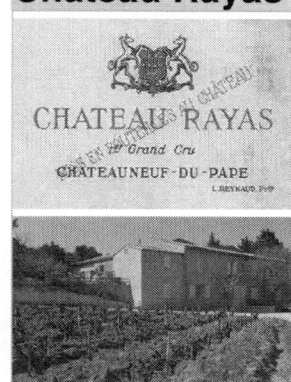

Route de Courthézon, 84230 Châteauneuf-du-Pape

33) 04 90 83 73 09 (33) 04 90 65 41 75

Emmanuel Reynaud

(33) 04 90 65 38 46 et +33(0)4 90 83 51 17

www.chateaurayas.fr

Châteauneuf-du-Pape

Châteauneuf-du-Pape, Pignan

13 ha; 20,000 bottles
[map p. 32]

Château Rayas is a legend, not just for the quality of its wine, but for the idiosyncratic behavior of its proprietors. The British importer used to tell the story of how he turned up for a visit to find the place deserted, and then as he was driving away, saw Louis Reynaud climbing out of the ditch where he had been hiding. Two proprietors later (after Rayas passed on to Louis's son Jacques and then to Jacques's nephew Emmanuel), it is still difficult to arrange to visit Rayas, but when you get there, it turns out the stories are true about the contrast between the primitive old cellars and the quality of the wine. The "Château" is a utilitarian building on a small hill, in a slightly obscure location that is not so easy to find. Several rough holes have been knocked in the concrete floor that separates the two storeys, presumably to allow pipes to be run through.

There is no arguing with the quality of Rayas: the red is made exclusively from Grenache, but it does not slide over the edge into jamminess. The white Rayas, although less well known than the red, is equally remarkable, especially as it comes from a blend of the undistinguished Grenache Blanc with Clairette: it has a wonderful savory quality, redolent of the garrigue of the south.

Rayas has several individual vineyards, each surrounded by the local forest. Next to the Château is the "Coeur" vineyard. The terroir is sandy and a slight elevation relative to the surrounding countryside ensures breezes that give freshness. The other major plots are the Couchant (to the west) and the Levant (to the east). All the plantings are Grenache. A little to the north is the Pignan area, used to produce the second wine, called after the area. The vines date back about 70 years, and are replaced individually as necessary; there is never any wholesale replanting.

Barrel samples provide an unusual opportunity to directly compare different expressions of Grenache. Coeur is silky, refined and sophisticated rather than fleshy. Le Couchant is warmer and nuttier (more typically Grenache, you might say), rounder and richer, with a faint sweet impression on the finish. Le Levant is sterner: I felt this might provide the backbone for the blend. I could see these components combining to offer freshness, fruits, and structure, but the whole is undoubtedly greater than the sum of the parts in the magic that is Rayas. Emmanuel is not especially forthcoming about his techniques, so I was not really able to establish his opinion on how these features contribute to Rayas's ability to retain freshness so well.

But there is something of a split personality here, because Château de Fonsalette, a medium size property in the Côtes du Rhône, is also owned and made at Rayas (and a remarkable price it is too, for a Côtes du Rhône). And under the same ownership is the much larger Château des Tours, where a Vacqueyras is made from Grenache and Syrah, and a Côtes du Rhône from a blend of Grenache with Cinsault and Syrah. Perhaps the cobwebs are for show.

Domaine Roger Sabon ★★

Avenue Impérial BP 57, 84230 Châteauneuf-du-Pape

(33) 04 90 83 71 72

Gilbert Sabon

@ contact@roger-sabon.com

www.domainerogersabon.com

Châteauneuf-du-Pape

Châteauneuf-du-Pape, Réserve

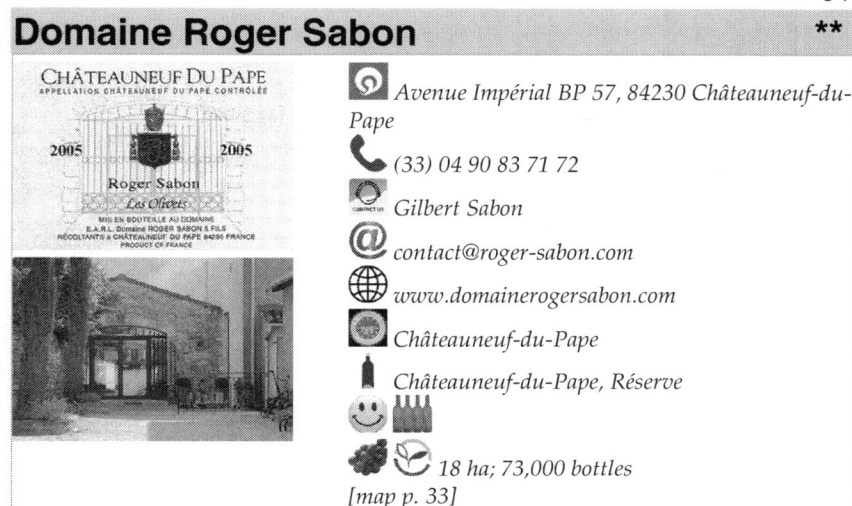

18 ha; 73,000 bottles
[map p. 33]

Séraphin Sabon was making wine at the start of the twentieth century, and this domain was founded in 1952 by his son Roger Sabon with 15 ha of Châteauneuf-du-Pape. Today the vineyards fall into 13 separate parcels, and also include holdings in Lirac and Côtes du Rhône.

Production focuses on reds: the 5% of white production is vinified in one large wooden cask. The Côtes du Rhône and also a Vin de France are fermented in cement and made to be fruity and easy to drink. Lirac and Châteauneuf-du-Pape are fermented in stainless steel. The wine rests six months in cuve, then after assemblage is matured in foudres or demi-muids for a year. "Our approach is a little different in that each cuvée has a style and we try to maintain that style each year. It's not necessarily the same parcels in each cuvée every year," says winemaker Didier Negron.

Three cuvées are made in roughly equal amounts. With Les Olivets, the objective is to have a traditional wine that's ready to drink soon; it is 80% Grenache, 10% Syrah, and 10% Cinsault. The Réserve is richer and more structured, and Prestige is more powerful, intended to be a vin de garde. These were among the first special cuvées made in Châteauneuf (in 1981 and 1982), and were received with some suspicion at the time. In addition there is Le Secret des Sabon, a special cuvée coming from hundred-year-old vines planted by Séraphin Sabon. There's increasing power going up the scale; I like the balance of Réserve best.

Domaine Saint Préfert *

425 Chemin Saint Préfert, 84230 Châteauneuf-du-Pape

(33) 04 90 83 75 03

Isabel Ferrando

contact@st-prefert.fr

www.st-prefert.fr

Châteauneuf-du-Pape

Châteauneuf du Pape, August Favier

Châteauneuf du Pape

28 ha; 32,000 bottles [map p. 32]

Isabel Ferrando made a stir with the release of her first vintage, 2003, after she left a career as a banker with Crédite Agricole to purchase Domaine Saint Préfert. The domain had 13 ha in the area of Serres in the south where the stony terroir is based on the galets; it was founded by Fernand Serre in the 1930s (chosen because the lieu-dit had his name), but after his death his family somewhat lost interest.

Isabel has been expanding ever since the purchase. Henri Bonneau became her mentor and helped with replanting. The old vines (average age 60 years), including some other varieties intermingled with Grenache, are being perpetuated by selection massale. A new cellar was built in 2009, based on the modernist principles of the Bauhaus, which seems appropriate for the domain.

Several cuvées are bottled under St Préfert, and there is also a single cuvée bottled as Domaine Isabel Ferrando, based on old vines Grenache in the Colombis lieu-dit where the terroir is sandier and some other plots: the change in label is intended to emphasize the difference in terroir.

The domain Châteauneuf comes from younger vines and is 85% Grenache; it ages in cement. Cuvée Auguste Favier comes from Serres and is largely Grenache (mostly aged in cement) with other varieties (Syrah, Cinsault, and Mourvèdre) aged in old demi-muids. The impressive feature is that the richness of the palate is offset by a touch of minerality, and the wine really remains fresh. Charles Giraud is 60% Grenache with 35% Mourvèdre and 5% Syrah from the oldest vines, aged in demi-muids. The domain changed from destemming to whole cluster fermentation in 2009. Refined is not a word I often use in conjunction with Châteauneuf, but it is appropriate here. The white, a blend of 85% Clairette with 15% Roussanne, is as refined as the red, and has achieved a great reputation. There is also a Côtes du Rhône from the area of Sorgues.

Château Sixtine

10 Route de Courthézon, 84230 Châteauneuf-du-Pape

(33) 04 90 83 70 51

Jean-Marc Diffonty

contact@chateau-sixtine.com

www.chateau-sixtine.com

Châteauneuf-du-Pape

Châteauneuf-du-Pape

22 ha; 300,000 bottles

[map p. 33]

This is a family domain, owned by the Diffonty family. Jean-Marc Diffonty made many changes when he took charge in the 1990s, after his father called him to come and take over, although he had not intended to run the domain. From the road the premises look relatively small, but there is surprisingly large complex of warehouse-like buildings behind the façade. The winery was refurbished in 2003.

Before the second world war, everything was sold in bulk, much of it to Burgundy! Bottling started here in 1952. The wine was sold as the Cuvée du Vatican. Jean-Marc wanted to distinguish the wine of the estate, and since 2010 the domain wines have been labeled as Château Sixtine, and Cuvée de Vatican has been used for negociant wines. Sixtine is about a quarter of total production, with 10% white.

Vineyards are dispersed around the appellation. Jean-Marc has moved away from the traditional dominance of Grenache, and the Château Sixtine red is 45% Grenache, 30% Mourvèdre, and 25% Syrah, aged in a mix of cuve and wood. One intention is to give some longevity to the wine. "The Cuvée du Vatican Châteauneuf is more typical of the appellation than Château Sixtine as it has 70% Grenache, 20% Syrah, and 10% Mourvèdre," is the view at the domaine.

Under Cuvée du Vatican there are all three colors of Côtes du Rhône, a red Côtes du Rhône Village, and a Châteauneuf-du-Pape. The Cotes du Rhône are pleasant, but not very characterful. The Châteauneuf follows the same light style.

The intention is to make a red and white for Château Sixtine. "Château Sixtine is the grand vin. I decided to make the wine like Bordeaux, I don't want to make micro-cuvées," Jean-Marc says. The white is 95% Roussanne with 5% Clairette and aged in barriques. It makes a classy impression with a faintly savory style. There's selection to make the red grand vin, with rejected lots going into the negociant wine. The style aims at elegance rather than power.

Domaine de La Solitude **

Route de Bédarrides, 84231 Châteauneuf-du-Pape

(33) 04 90 83 71 45

Florent Lançon

info@domaine-solitude.com

www.domaine-solitude.com

Châteauneuf-du-Pape

Châteauneuf-du-Pape

37 ha; 300,000 bottles

[map p. 32]

One of the oldest domains in Châteauneuf-du-Pape, La Solitude was purchased as a dowry for marriage into the Barberini family, which changed its name to Barberin in Châteauneuf in 1604. The wine was being sold as Vin de la Solitude before the French Revolution, and the domain claims to have been bottling its own wine by 1815. The domain is still run by direct descendants of the Barberin family. Florent Lançon is the eight generation, and takes over from his father, Jean-Michel, in 2019.

This is now a sizeable domain, with 38 ha in Châteauneuf, all in a single block to the east of the town. Côtes du Rhône comes from local growers. "We used to own some Côtes du Rhône, but we sold them to focus exclusively on viticulture in Châteauneuf," Florent says. "There are lots of good growers in the area, but they don't know how to make or sell wine. So we've worked with them for Côtes du Rhône since 2013." Châteauneuf-du-Pape is a third of total production.

"We are known for freshness and balance for the whites, finesse and elegance for the reds," is how Florent summarized the domain. "All wines are around 13% alcohol." The Côtes du Rhône is a GSM, aged in concrete, and elegant rather than powerful. "I want it to be accessible and drink well for 3-5 years."

Plantings in Châteauneuf are a little unusual. Whites are almost a quarter, based on Grenache Blanc and Roussanne, with a little Clairette and Bourboulenc. Red plantings are about 50% Grenache, 20% Syrah, 10% Mourvèdre, with small amounts of the other varieties. Grenache is usually intermingled with another variety in the vineyard. Usually there are around 65,000 bottles of red, 20,000 of white, and 15,000 for various special cuvées, which are made most years. "You might say we have too many cuvées, but each one is different, and there's a history, and they are made in small proportions only in the best vintages," Florent explains.

Cuvée Barberini is made in both red (80% Grenache) and white (80% Roussanne). The style is quite rich and classic. Cornelia Constanza comes from the oldest vineyard, just opposite the winery — "this was my jungle when I was a child" — planted just after phylloxera. Made only in best vintages, it is 100% Grenache, with 30% whole clusters. It has all the concentration of old vines Grenache, yet shows that refined palate characteristic of the house. Réserve Secrète is a blend of selected lots of very old Grenache and old Syrah; when young the Grenache dominates, but as it ages the Syrah becomes more evident, and it will easily last 20-30 years. Vin de Solitude is an interesting project to make a wine with the blend like it was before phylloxera; with much less Grenache, it is much lighter than a modern cuvée. The overall impression of the house style is clean and pure; if I had to choose a single word to describe it, it would be "silky."

Domaine Pierre Usseglio   **

10 Route d'Orange, 84230 Châteauneuf-du-Pape

(33) 04 90 83 72 98

Thierry Usseglio

info@domainepierreusseglio.fr

www.domainepierreusseglio.fr

Châteauneuf-du-Pape

Châteauneuf-du-Pape

28 ha; 80,000 bottles

[map p. 33]

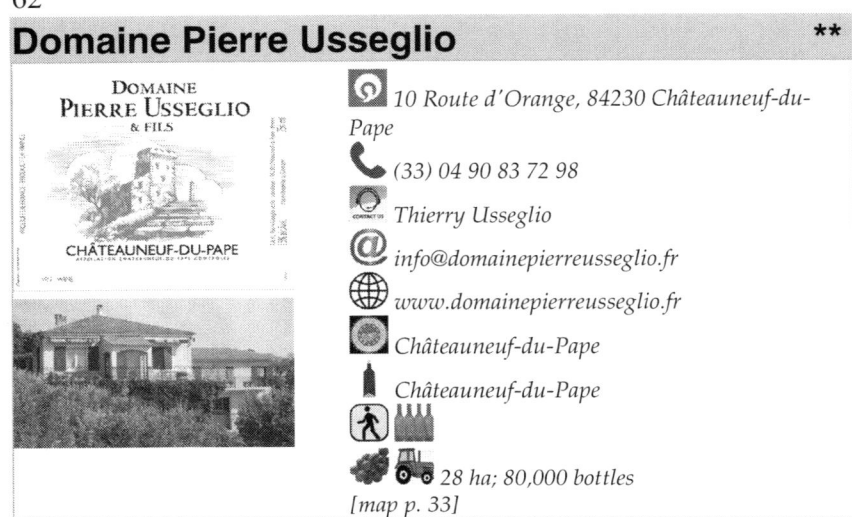

Francis Usseglio came from Piedmont in 1931 and started producing wine from leased vineyards in 1948. His son Pierre took over and purchased plots to establish Domaine Pierre Usseglio in 1966. Pierre's brother Raymond established another domain, Domaine Raymond Usseglio, shortly after (see mini-profile). Now with 17 vineyard parcels in three separate areas of the appellation, with half of the vines older than eighty years, Domaine Pierre Usseglio is presently run by brothers Jean-Pierre and Thierry.

There are regular cuvées of both red and white Châteauneuf-du-Pape (called Cuvée Traditionelle), the Réserve des Deux Frères which is a selection of lots, usually 70% Grenache and 30% Syrah, aged in a mixture of foudres and barriques, and the cuvée that made the domain famous, the Cuvée de Mon Aïeul, which was introduced in 1998 from a 2 ha plot planted in 1926. (Subsequently some grapes have also been sourced from other plots.) This is a Grenache-dominated cuvée (usually 90% today), enormously rich and dense, matured in a mix of wood and stainless steel.

All of the wines of the domain show strong Grenache influence, in a modern style, but the Cuvée de Mon Aïeul is the über-Châteauneuf, with forceful, high-toned aromatics. The focus on super-richness was reinforced in 2007 by the Not for You cuvée from a single barrique coming from 95-year-old Grenache vines. The domain has expanded and there are now also wines from Lirac, Côtes du Rhône, and Vin de France.

Domaine de La Vieille Julienne ★

Domaine de La Vieille Julienne 2007

◉ Route de Courthézon le Gres, 84100 Orange
📞 (33) 04 90 34 20 10
✉ Jean-Paul Daumen
@ contact@vieillejulienne.com
🌐 www.vieillejulienne.com
🍷 Châteauneuf-du-Pape
🍾 Châteauneuf-du-Pape
15 ha; 40,000 bottles
[map p. 32]

The domain was created in 1905, but did not begin bottling until the 1960s. Jean-Paul Daumen, the fourth generation, took over in the 1990s. Located to the north, the 10 ha of vineyards in Châteauneuf-du-Pape are in three blocks at the edge of the appellation. There are also 5 ha in the Côtes du Rhône.

Grapes are destemmed, vinified in concrete, and matured in foudres. Until recently, there were only two cuvées of Châteauneuf-du-Pape: the regular bottling and Le Réservé, made only in some years (when the oldest vines—more than a hundred years old Grenache—achieve something special, says Jean-Paul). Since 2012 there have also been wines based on selection. "I still pick parcels separately, but I make a true parcel selection for my wines, versus just blends," Jean-Paul explains. Les Trois Sources comes from two areas (clay-limestone and galets); Les Haut Lieux comes from the more elevated vineyards.

Like the Châteauneuf, the Côtes du Rhône is dominated by old Grenache; it comes from vineyards in the lieu-dit Clavin just over the border from the vineyards in Châteauneuf-du-Pape (literally on the other side of the D72). There is no white Châteauneuf, but there is a white Côtes du Rhône, which includes grapes from the small amount of white plantings in Châteauneuf. In addition, there's a negociant business under the Daumen name (which includes declassified lots from young vines at Vieille Julienne as well as those purchased from other sources).

Domaine Le Vieux Donjon *

Route de Courthézon, 84232 Châteauneuf-du-Pape

(33) 044 90 83 70 03

Claire Fabre

contact@levieuxdonjon.fr

www.levieuxdonjon.com

Châteauneuf-du-Pape

Châteauneuf-du-Pape

15 ha; 50,000 bottles
[map p. 66]

A relatively recent domain, Vieux Donjon originated when Marcel Michel started estate-bottling in 1966, but took its present form from the combination of vineyards from two families after the marriage of Marie José and Lucien Michel in 1979. Mostly in the northern part of the appellation on the galets, with the rest on sandier soils in the south, the vineyards have been in the families for generations, and include a good proportion of very old Grenache vines. The vineyards include one hectare of white grapes. The domain is now run by the next generation, Marie José and Lucien's daughter Claire Fabre.

The philosophy of the domain remains quite traditional, and there is only a single red and a single white wine; Vieux Donjon is one of the few prominent houses that have withstood the trend to special cuvées. The red has a more or less average mix of 75% Grenache, 10% Syrah, 10% Mourvèdre, and 5% Cinsault. The white is 50% Grenache Blanc with the rest from Clairette, Bourboulenc, and a little Roussanne. Vinification is traditional, with grapes partially destemmed and all varieties fermented together in concrete tanks, followed by maturation in foudres. There is no new oak.

This is very reliable, mainstream Châteauneuf-du-Pape, solid and sturdy, sometimes described as old school; it's always a safe bet in a restaurant, although it does not usually rise to the heights. The wine is recognized as one of the better values from the appellation.

Domaine du Vieux Télégraphe ***

3, Route Châteauneuf-du-Pape, 84370 Bédarrides

(33) 04 90 33 00 31

Daniel Brunier

vignobles@brunier.fr

www.vignoblesbrunier.fr

Châteauneuf-du-Pape

Châteauneuf-du-Pape, La Crau

72 ha; 280,000 bottles

[map p. 32]

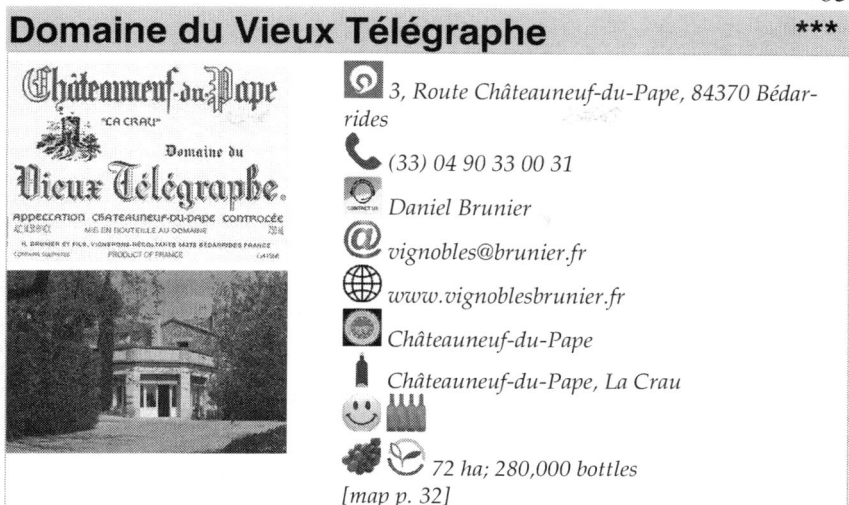

The heart of Vieux Télégraphe is the vineyard on the stony soil of the La Crau plateau in the southeastern part of the appellation. Production follows classic lines, with 90% red and 10% white. Established by Hippolyte Brunier in 1898, this remains a family business, today run by Daniel Brunier and his brother. The Bruniers also own Domaine La Roquette (bought in 1986), which has 30 ha in the more western parts of Châteauneuf, including the stony Plateau de Pielong and the sandy Pignan district. In addition, they bought Les Pallières in Gigondas in partnership with Kermit Lynch, and they make wine in Ventoux.

All production is from their estates. "Oh no, we don't want to expand into the negociant business, we are growers, it's so frustrating to buy grapes and wines," says Daniel Brunier. The philosophy is to produce a single wine for each domain. There is a joint second wine, Télégramme, for Vieux Télégraphe and La Roquette, made from young vines or occasional declassified cuvées. The red Vieux Télégraphe has 65% Grenache, 15% Mourvèdre, 15% Syrah, and 5% Cinsault, from vines with an average age of 50 years. The red wines of both domains are made by fermentation in stainless steel, transfer to concrete tanks for 9 months, and maturation in foudres of old oak for 8-12 months. The wines are neither fined nor filtered. Vieux Télégraphe is distinguished by a restraint that allows graceful aging for years: the 1985 was still vibrant when I visited in 2013.

Gigondas-Vacqueyras-Beaumes de Venise

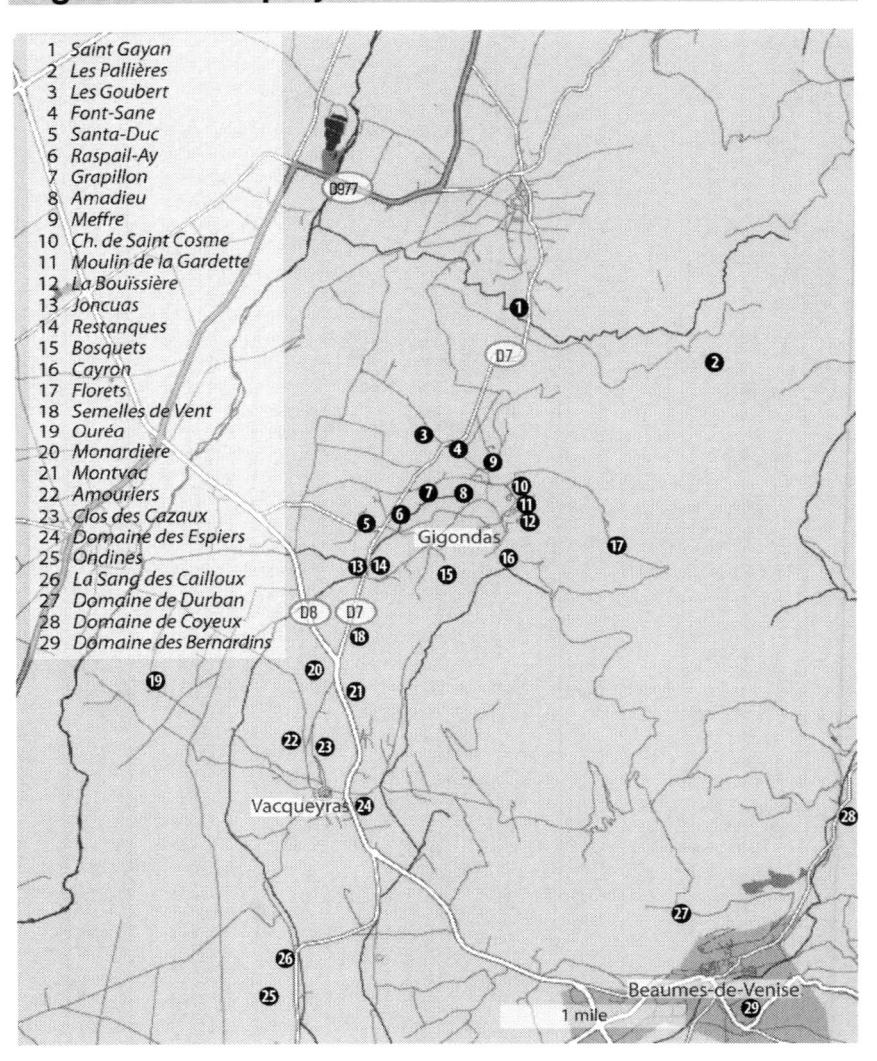

1. Saint Gayan
2. Les Pallières
3. Les Goubert
4. Font-Sane
5. Santa-Duc
6. Raspail-Ay
7. Grapillon
8. Amadieu
9. Meffre
10. Ch. de Saint Cosme
11. Moulin de la Gardette
12. La Bouïssière
13. Joncuas
14. Restanques
15. Bosquets
16. Cayron
17. Florets
18. Semelles de Vent
19. Ouréa
20. Monardière
21. Montvac
22. Amouriers
23. Clos des Cazaux
24. Domaine des Espiers
25. Ondines
26. La Sang des Cailloux
27. Domaine de Durban
28. Domaine de Coyeux
29. Domaine des Bernardins

Pierre Amadieu

201 Route des Princes d'Orange, 84190 Gigondas

(33) 04 90 65 84 08

Pierre Amadieu

contact@pierre-amadieu.com

www.pierre-amadieu.com

Gigondas

137 ha; 600,000 bottles

[map p. 66]

This negociant house became famous in 1929 when Pierre Amadieu started to bottle Gigondas from his 7 ha of vineyards. Finding the supply insufficient, he also became a negociant. Located at the foot of the village, that 7 ha remains the core of the house, but has now been greatly expanded. In fact, just before the cooperative was established (in 1956) as a competitor for grapes, Pierre Amadieu purchased the 400 ha domain of Grand Romane et La Machotte (covering 10% of the Gigondas appellation), on which he planted another 65 ha of vineyards. In the hands of the third generation today—Pierre is in charge of winemaking and his uncle Claude manages the vineyards—the house is the largest single producer of Gigondas from its own and purchased grapes. You can't miss the tasting room on the road going up into Gigondas village.

Winemaking is traditional, with most of each wine aged in foudres, the rest in barriques. Romane Machotte is the basic Gigondas, 80% Grenache and 20% Syrah. It has a sturdy style, while Grand Romane is a GSM and is a little tauter. The top wine is the Pas de l'Aigle single vineyard selection of 90% Grenache and 10% Syrah; coming from high up in the Dentelles, this is more restrained and sophisticated. Within Gigondas there is a large plot of old vines Clairette, but the white is sold as Côtes du Rhône as the Gigondas AOP does not include whites. Amadieu also produces wines from other appellations in the southern and the northern Rhône. The wines are well regarded for their consistent quality.

Domaine des Bernardins *

138, Avenue Gambetta, 84190 Beaumes de Venise

(33) 04 90 62 94 13

Elisabeth Hall

contact@domaine-des-bernardins.com

www.domaine-des-bernardins.com

Beaumes de Venise

IGP Vaucluse, Doré des Bernardins

Beaumes de Venise, Hommage

25 ha; 100,000 bottles

[map p. 66]

The domain takes its name from the Bernardin monks who used to own the property. It's been in the hands of the Castaud family for five generations, since the nineteenth century (they still have a bottle of Muscat from 1847 in the wine library). Louis Castaud was involved in obtaining appellation status for Beaumes de Venise in 1955, and today the domain is run by his granddaughter Elisabeth together with her husband Andrew Hall. The tasting room is located right in the town.

Production is about three quarters Muscat Beaumes de Venise, coming from plantings of three quarters Muscat à Petits Grains Blanc and one quarter Muscat à Petit Grains Noir. In addition to the regular bottling, there's a multivintage cuvée called Hommage. The name is intended to imply homage to the style of wine Louis Castaud used to produce in the 1930s: rich, full, dark, and intense in an oxidative style. The youngest wines in the blend are five years old. With a perfumed nose, and impressions of caramel on the palate, I find it more intense and interesting than the regular vintage cuvée.

When production is sufficient, there may also be a dry Muscat cuvée (an IGP) called Le Doré des Bernardins (the grapes are harvested together with those for the sweet wine, but fermentation is allowed to proceed to completion). The dry Muscat is quite flavorful, and more interesting than most. Red wine for the Beaumes de Venise and Côtes du Rhône comes from 8 ha planted with Grenache, Syrah, Cinsault, and Mourvèdre; there are also some white grapes mixed with the red. The reds are quite soft, dominated by impressions of Grenache. There is also a Grenache-based rosé.

Domaine La Bouïssière

15 Rue du Portail, 84190 Gigondas
(33) 04 90 65 87 91
Thierry Faravel
labouissiere@aol.com
Gigondas
Gigondas

17 ha; 45,000 bottles
[map p. 66]

Thierry Faravel and his brother Gilles run this domain, which was created by their father in 1978. The first vines had been planted earlier, when Antonin Faravel was chef de culture at the negociant Amadieu, and he worked on the plot at weekends, selling grapes to Amadieu until he started the domain. Just over half the vineyards today are in Gigondas, almost all at relatively high elevations in the Dentelles, with the rest in Vacqueyras, Beaumes de Venise (black plantings, but sold to the cooperative), and also some plantings for Vin de France. The winery is in a small building (looking like an ordinary garage from the outside) on the outskirts of Gigondas, with a small tasting room in the town.

The wines tend to a solid rich, ripe impression, with the Gigondas showing a little more restraint and increase in refinement over the Vacqueyras. "What is important for me is the typicity of the traditional cuvée as that represents the house," Thierry says. The cuvée Font de Tonin is a prestige cuvée from older vines, with a tighter balance that is really refined for Gigondas; there are usually around 400 cases, but it is not made every year. Part of the difference is due to the fact that the traditional cuvées are blends of Grenache and Syrah, but the Font de Tonin is a blend of Grenache and Mourvèdre. Also, the traditional cuvées are matured in foudres—Thierry has moved back to foudres to preserve the fruit better—but with its greater weight, the Font de Tonin remains in barriques.

Domaine du Cayron *

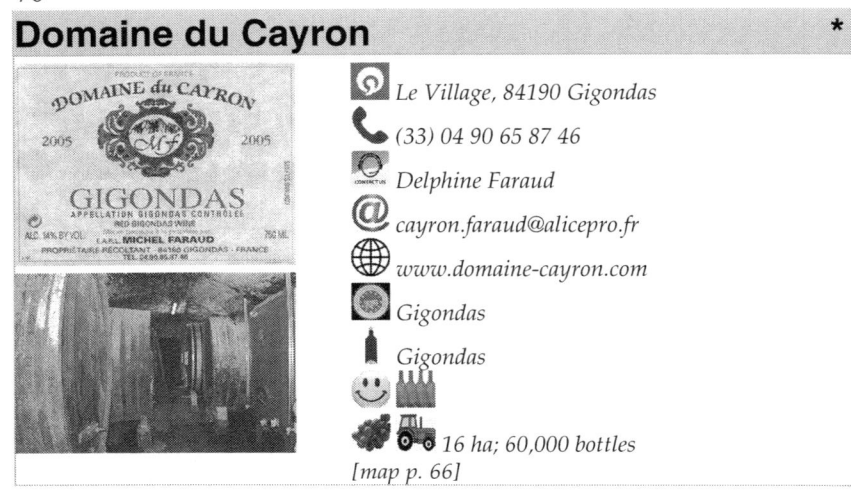

Le Village, 84190 Gigondas
(33) 04 90 65 87 46
Delphine Faraud
cayron.faraud@alicepro.fr
www.domaine-cayron.com
Gigondas
Gigondas
16 ha; 60,000 bottles
[map p. 66]

Founded in 1840, and until recently run by Michel Faraud for thirty years, the domain is now run by three sisters, Roseline, Delphine, and Cendrine Faraud, who are the fifth generation. It's located in a small utilitarian building in the main street of the village of Gigondas, with cramped cellars.

The vineyards in Gigondas are spread over twenty separate parcels, with an average vine age of 45 years. Usually individual vines are replaced as necessary, but the highest vineyard in the Dentelles, on the Côte du Cayron, has been pulled out, and new terraces are being constructed for replanting. The domain has 70% Grenache, 14% Syrah, 11% Cinsault, and a little Mourvèdre.

The policy has been consistent for decades: only a single cuvée is made. This is widely regarded as a domain whose wines define the classic traditions of Gigondas. "We do traditional vinification with vendange entière, everything goes through alcoholic then malolactic fermentation, pressing with an old bench press, and assemblage more or less directly after the MLF in February. Everything goes into foudres for 12 months," Delphine says. The foudres are quite old, although two were replaced in 2011: this makes for a slight increase in freshness compared with samples from the old foudres. For all the reputation for tradition (most commentators refer to the massive structure and richness of the wine), I find the sense of precision and elegance quite evident from foudre samples to finished wine.

Domaine le Clos des Cazaux *

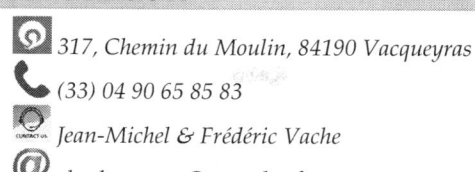

317, Chemin du Moulin, 84190 Vacqueyras

(33) 04 90 65 85 83

Jean-Michel & Frédéric Vache

closdescazaux@wanadoo.fr

www.closdescazaux.fr

Vacqueyras

Vacqueyras, Cuvée Saint Roch

48 ha; 120,000 bottles
[map p. 66]

This family estate is now run by brothers Jean-Michel and Frédéric Vache. The building has a slightly shabby appearance, with old enameled tanks at the entrance, and a small bottling line in the back. Almost all the vineyards have been in the family for the past fifty years; more than half are in Vacqueyras, with some in Gigondas; there are also some Côtes du Rhône and Vin de France. Plantings are similar in Vacqueyras and Gigondas, with 50-60% Grenache, lots of Syrah, and a little Mourvèdre.

"The Syrah was planted in Gigondas in the sixties when grandfather created the vineyard, but in Vacqueyras we've been replacing a lot of the Grenache with Syrah," says Jean-Michel, who is really concerned about the effects of warmer vintages. "We are making wine to match food, so our objective is to get balance, always balance, we are frightened by alcohol. A good balance for a Grenache-based wine is 13.5%, 14% maximum, and a good balance for a Syrah wine is 13-13.5%. To make outstanding wine at 15% is really rare," he says.

There are pleasing herbal overtones to the cuvées Saint Roch and des Templiers from Vacqueyras, and La Tour Sarrasine from Gigondas. The focus on Syrah has brought an unusual degree of refinement to the Cuvée des Templiers. Up one step, the Prestige cuvée from Gigondas comes from old vines of Grenache; and the Grenat Noble from Vacqueyras is a rare sweet Grenache with botrytis (made every three or four years).

Domaine de Coyeux *

Route de Lafare, 84190 Beaumes de Venise
(33) 04 90 12 42 42
Yves Nativelle
coyeux.nativelle@wanadoo.fr
Beaumes de Venise
Beaumes de Venise
120 ha; 350,000 bottles
[map p. 66]

The domain has one of the most spectacular views in the region, with vineyards at an average altitude of 260m at the foot of the Dentelles de Montmirail, overlooking the town of Beaumes de Venise. Yves and Catherine Nativelle started with the purchase of a 7 ha estate in 1976, and continued to add vineyards, building up the domain to comprise one of the largest estates in the area, all in a contiguous block. The soil is an outcrop of Trias (deep soils of decomposed rocks, rich in iron).

Most of the plantings are Muscat, and the focus is really on the dessert wine, which is the most important single product. The first Muscat de Beaumes de Venise was produced in 1982; in fact, the production of Muscat de Beaumes de Venise (including the cuvée Les Trois Fonts) accounts for around 10% of the total production of the appellation.

Besides Muscat, the other plantings are black grapes, consisting of 50% Grenache, 20% Syrah, 20% Mourvèdre, and 10% Cinsault, used to produce red Beaumes de Venise, Gigondas, and Côtes du Rhône Villages. There's also a dry Muscat, labeled as IGP Méditerranée.

The domain stands out as one of the relatively few to produce estate-bottled wine in Beaumes de Venise (most wine in the appellation is produced by negociants). There is no mistaking the character of the Muscat, but the style of the wine is relatively light and straightforward. Like all Muscat, it's best drunk young, within a couple of years of the vintage

Domaine de Durban

Leydier, 84190 Beaumes de Venise
(33) 04 90 62 94 26
Henri Leydier
contact@domainedurban.com
www.domainedurban.com

Beaumes de Venise
Beaumes de Venise, Cuvée Prestige
Beaumes de Venise

33 ha; 250,000 bottles [map p. 66]

Situated above the town of Beaumes de Venise with a panoramic view over the vineyards, the domain is best known for its sweet Muscat de Beaumes de Venise, but it also produces dry red wine from Beaumes de Venise and from neighboring Gigondas, varietal white wines of Chardonnay and Viognier in the IGP Vaucluse, and rosé. Jacques Leydier bought the property (which according to records going back to 1159 had been a fortified farm in the Middle Ages) in a state of complete disrepair in 1960; today it is run by his grandsons, Henri and Philippe. The soils are a mixture of Trias (an unusual soil type, very rich in iron, that's characteristic of the area) and clay-limestone. Production is split more or less equally between sweet wine and dry wine.

Beaumes de Venise can be made only from Muscat à Petits Grains Blanc or Noir, and the Leydiers believe that the quality of their Muscat partly derives from the fact that the domain grows only Muscat à Petits Grains Blanc. It may also be a factor that most vineyards are located lower down, on the plain, and Domaine de Durban is one of the few above the village. The VDN is vinified in stainless steel, neutral spirits are added to stop fermentation with 110 g/l of residual sugar—"we stop at the minimum so the won won't become cloying"—and the wine is matured in cuve for about five months until it is bottled. Domaine de Durban is widely considered to produce the best sweet wine of the appellation. There is only a single cuvée; it's a distinctive style, more perfumed than grapey, and one of the few to have character instead of sweetness.

The Beaumes de Venise red is fermented in stainless steel and aged in concrete to produce a soft, attractive wine. The latest cuvée is the Prestige, which is the same GSM blend but is aged in barriques. The wood brings a certain sense of austerity. The Gigondas comes from just over the hill and has more sense of structure, but follows the house style. "This is an atypical Gigondas, because it rests on the fruits," says Henri Leydier.

Domaine des Espiers *

Route de Vaison la Romaine, 84190 Vacqueyras
(33) 04 90 65 81 16
Philippe Cartoux
p.cartoux@free.fr
domaine-des-espiers.com
Vacqueyras
Gigondas
11 ha; 50,000 bottles
[map p. 66]

Philippe Cartoux created this domain in 1989 with 2 ha in an area where his family had owned vines in the nineteenth century, and then built it up by further purchases. For the first few years the wine was sold to negociants, until Philippe felt it was good enough to bottle under the estate name. The vineyards are planted with two thirds Grenache and one third Syrah (with a little Mourvèdre), producing Gigondas (3 ha), and Côtes du Rhône Sablet (2.5 ha), and Côtes du Rhône (4 ha) from vineyards in Violès. Vines are planted at higher density than usual for the area (5,400 vines per hectare compared to the normal 3,500).

The Gigondas and Côtes du Rhône Sablet are blends exclusively of Grenache and Syrah; the Mourvèdre goes into the Côtes du Rhône (both red and rosé). The focus is on red wine, but there, is a white Côtes du Rhône (50% Roussanne and 50% Clairette) from a small plot in Sablet. Côtes du Rhône Sablet is vinified in cement cuves. There are two cuvées of Gigondas. Les Grames comes from an area on the plain and is aged in concrete; Les Bâches comes from older vines near the foot of the Dentelles and is matured in demi muids. It is harvested at super-ripeness, and uses higher fermentation temperatures to get maximum extraction. Going up the range, there's more sense of structure and greater refinement, with Les Bâches seeming more modern than Les Grames.

Philippe is married to Cécile Dusserre of Domaine de Montvac (see profile), and the wines are made there. As there is no cave at Violès, the wines can be tasted at Montvac.

Domaine de Montvac

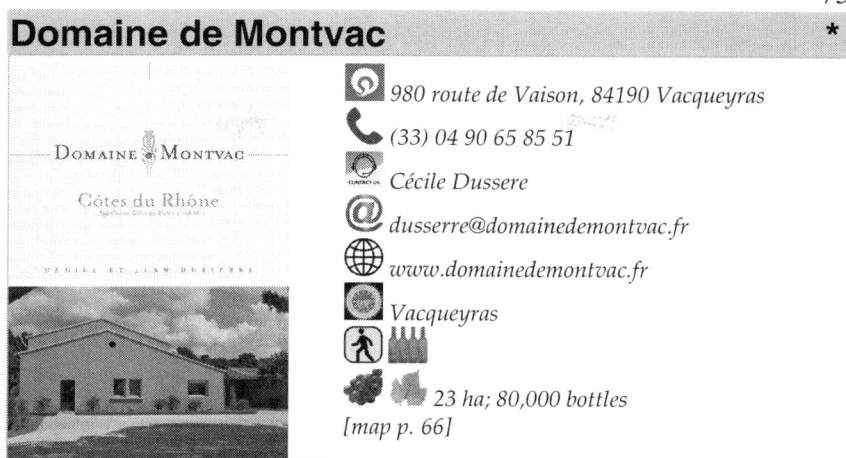

980 route de Vaison, 84190 Vacqueyras
(33) 04 90 65 85 51
Cécile Dussere
dusserre@domainedemontvac.fr
www.domainedemontvac.fr
Vacqueyras

23 ha; 80,000 bottles
[map p. 66]

This matriarchal domain has been handed down from mother to daughter for five generations, and is set to continue. The family started as tonneliers and slowly bought vineyards, eventually becoming entirely vignerons. The majority of vineyards (20 ha) are in Vacqueyras, with some plots in Gigondas and Côtes du Rhône. Small plots are spread all around the appellations. The Côtes du Rhône red and rosé come from grapes that are mostly (95%) declassified from Vacqueyras and Gigondas. Production is almost entirely red; white is only 3%.

The Mélodine white from Vacqueyras comes from four varieties, Clairette, Roussanne, Viognier, and Bourboulenc, that are planted together and cofermented. It makes quite a soft, fragrant impression. Reds are fermented and aged mostly in concrete. "We have only a little wood," Cécile Duserre says. "We only use pumping-over because we don't want to extract too much. We don't want to have over-maturity because we want to have natural acidity and show the purity of the fruits." Everything is destemmed.

The Côtes du Rhône previews the house style, with black fruits on the palate, and a slightly stern impression of the underlying structure. Vacqueyras Arabesque is an assemblage from parcels of many terroirs all over the appellation, while Variation comes from a parcel of 80-year-old Grenache (with a little Syrah) just behind the winery. Arabesque has a sense of tension, while the impressive concentration of old vines (achieving only 20 hl/ha) in Variation almost hides the chocolaty structure. Vincila is a selection of 60% old Grenache with 40% Syrah, has a year's longer aging, and offers a silky precision. The Gigondas comes from well up the Dentelles and makes a very fine impression in style between Arabesque and Vincila. The Gigondas and Vincila have some aging in demi-muids.

Domaine Les Pallières *

Route d'Encieu, 84190 Gigondas

(33) 04 90 65 85 07

Daniel Brunier

vignobles@brunier.fr

Gigondas

Gigondas, Terrasse du Diable

25 ha; 80,000 bottles
[map p. 66]

Les Pallières is a 135 ha estate, with 25 ha planted with vines in a natural amphitheater at elevations of 250-400m in the Dentelles. The underlying clay-sandy terroir is partially covered with calcareous rocks, becoming rockier with altitude. Owned by the Roux family for a century, originally the estate was planted with olive trees; subsequently they were replaced with grapevines. . About 80% of the vines are Grenache, but there's also some Syrah, Mourvèdre, Cinsault, and Clairette.

In 1998 the estate was purchased by a partnership between Domaine de Vieux Télégraphe of Châteauneuf-du-Pape and the American importer Kermit Lynch. About 5 ha were replanted, but the remainder are old vines. A new gravity-feed winery was constructed by 2002. The wine is made by the same team that produces Vieux Télégraphe.

There are two cuvées. Terrasse du Diable comes from 40-year old vines, running up to 400 m on a north-facing slope. Some white grapes are included. "The softening effect of Clairette (and some reduction in alcohol) is what we are looking for, and it brings some minerality," says Daniel Brunier of Vieux Télégraphe. Les Racines comes from 75-year-old vines and tends to have a more brooding presence, with an unusual sense of tension for a Grenache-based wine. It's one of the top wines from Gigondas (but in some vintages I prefer Terrasse du Diable for greater freshness.). There's also a rosé Vin de France, le Petit Bonheur.

Château de Saint Cosme *

📍 *126, Route des Florêts, 84190 Gigondas*
📞 *(33) 04 90 65 80 80*
✉ *Louis & Cherr Barruol*
@ *barruol@chateau-st-cosme.com*
🌐 *www.saintcosme.com*
▣ *Gigondas*
🍷 *Gigondas, Le Claux*

🍇 🛢 🍇 *22 ha; 120,000 bottles*
[map p. 66]

The Barruol family acquired Château de Saint Cosme in 1490; Louis Barruol is the fifteenth generation, and became involved as a student when his father was taken ill. Production was sold to negociants until Louis started estate bottling. The domain is more or less at the same elevation as Gigondas village, separated from it by a deep gully. The 15 ha of vineyards in Gigondas are all around, in small plots surrounded by the garrigue. There are also plots at Vinsobres in the Côtes du Rhône.

Saint Cosme is on a junction of two geological faults, so there are significant differences between individual vineyards. "We are a blending region, but given the geology of Saint Cosme it wouldn't be logical to blend all these sites," Louis says. so Saint Cosme is unusual in offering several bottlings from individual vineyards, all 100% Grenache from old vines. "There's no established tradition here, it's a pretty open debate whether you are for cuvées or lieu-dits. I've tried all my plots as separate wines. I keep those separate that work by themselves, but others can be good but need blending."

The entry-level wines are the Les Deux Albions cuvées, with a perfumed white showing Viognier's influence, and a red Côtes du Rhône dominated by Syrah. The Gigondas offers a mainstream representation of the appellation; the Valbelle cuvée is a blend of 80-year-old vines, including 10% Syrah as well as the predominant Grenache, from a mixture of terroirs, and gives more sense of restraint and finesse. The three single-vineyard wines show greater refinement, more sense of precision and minerality, rather than greater power. Le Claux is a 2 ha vineyard planted in 1870 on clay and limestone; it's deeper and more mineral than the Gigondas as such. Hominis Fides comes from a plot planted in 1902 on a terroir of limestone and sand, and reflects the terroir in a lighter, softer way. Le

Poste comes from vines that are a mere 75-years old on a limestone-marl terroir, and is more restrained but perhaps less concentrated than the others. All the cuvées have significant (30%) new oak, and once this wears off, offer a rare impression of the effects of terroir on Grenache.

Louis added a negociant business in 1997. Called "Négoce-Vigneron," it reflects Louis's wish to be a negociant "à l'ancienne," which is to say bringing the attitude of a grower to wines made from purchased grapes. The negociant wines are labeled simply as Saint Cosme (no Château). They include a Côtes du Rhône and all the cuvées from the northern Rhône except Cornas (see *Guide to Northern Rhône*).

Domaine Santa-Duc ✱

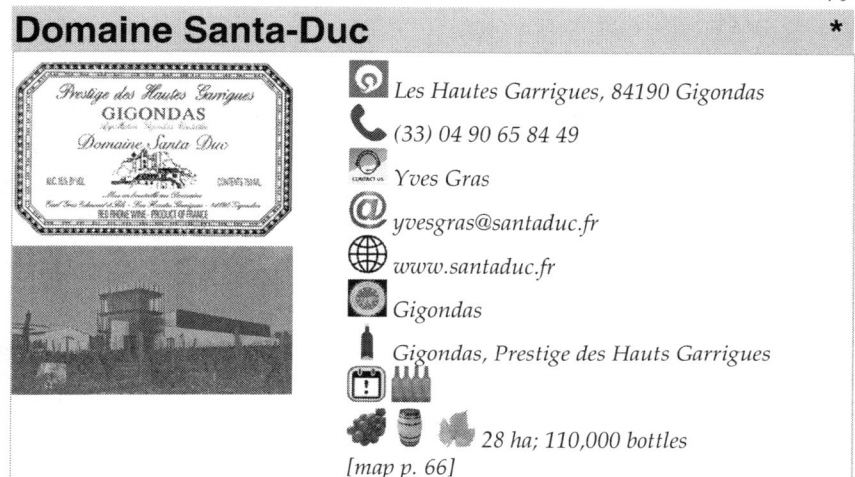

○ Les Hautes Garrigues, 84190 Gigondas
☏ (33) 04 90 65 84 49
 Yves Gras
@ yvesgras@santaduc.fr
⊕ www.santaduc.fr
 Gigondas
 Gigondas, Prestige des Hauts Garrigues
 28 ha; 110,000 bottles
[map p. 66]

Behind Santa-Duc's modern tasting room, located across the main road below the village of Gigondas, is a lively enterprise with a negociant activity as well as production of domain wines. Almost half the domain vineyards are in Gigondas, but there are also holdings in Vacqueyras, Rasteau, other parts of the Côtes du Rhône, and (most recently) Châteauneuf-du-Pape. "For twenty years I was a candidate to buy every plot that came up in Châteauneuf-du-Pape," says Yves Gras, who is the fifth generation at the domain.

Local character is expressed as freshness in the Côtes du Rhône Villages Roaix, which is quite classy for its appellation, there is a more robust impression in the Vacqueyras and Gigondas, and a sheen of finesse to the Châteauneuf-du-Pape. "My model looks to Burgundy with minerality and freshness, and good acidity," says Yves. "We are trying to keep alcohol levels down by picking earlier and changing grape handling," he adds, but the levels are now pushing 15%. However, the objective of retaining freshness has been achieved.

There are three cuvées from Gigondas: Tradition, Santa Roc (intended to be a fresher style), and Prestige du Garrigue (which comes from around the winery). The Prestige is an unconventional blend of Grenache with Mourvèdre: "They are very complementary because Grenache is oxidative and early, and Mourvèdre is reductive and late." The vines have a minimum age of 50 years and the wine is not made every year.

Côtes du Rhône

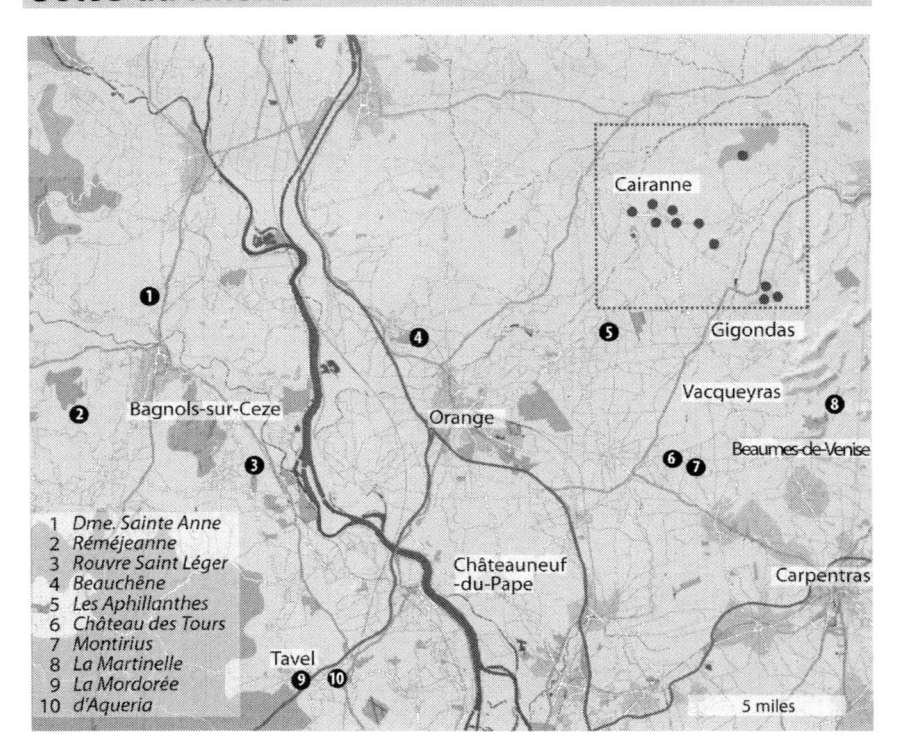

1 Dme. Sainte Anne
2 Réméjeanne
3 Rouvre Saint Léger
4 Beauchêne
5 Les Aphillanthes
6 Château des Tours
7 Montirius
8 La Martinelle
9 La Mordorée
10 d'Aqueria

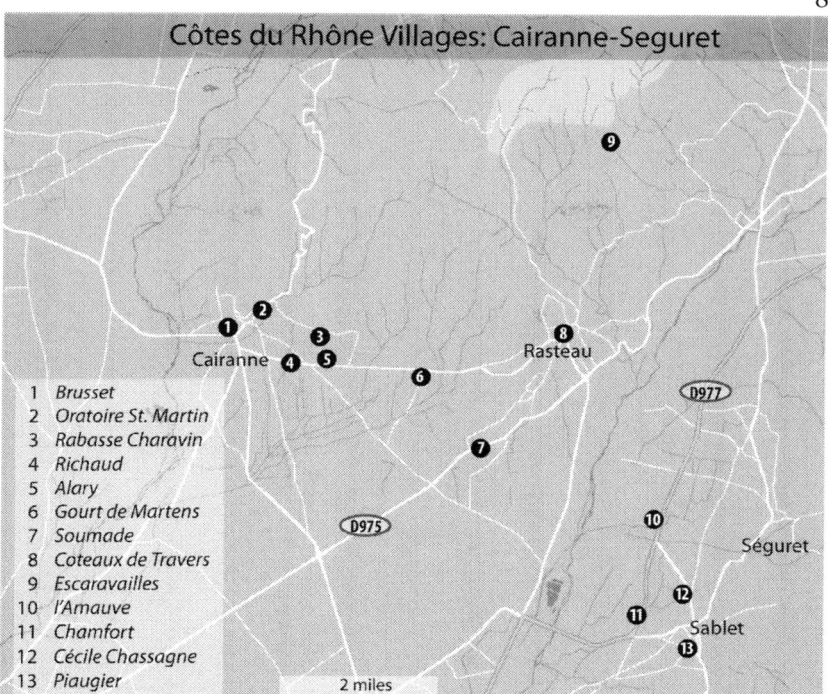

Côtes du Rhône Villages: Cairanne-Seguret

1 Brusset
2 Oratoire St. Martin
3 Rabasse Charavin
4 Richaud
5 Alary
6 Gourt de Martens
7 Soumade
8 Coteaux de Travers
9 Escaravailles
10 l'Amauve
11 Chamfort
12 Cécile Chassagne
13 Piaugier

Domaine Les Aphillanthes *

448 Chemin Saint-Jean, 84850 Travaillan

(33) 04 90 37 25 99

Héléne & Daniel Boulle

lesgalets84@wanadoo.fr

www.domainelesaphillanthes.fr

Côtes du Rhône

Côtes du Rhône, Plan de Dieu, Cuvée des Galets

55 ha; 100,000 bottles

[map p. 80]

Daniel Boulle is committed to the Côtes du Rhône, with ten or more different cuvées, including plain Côtes du Rhône, Côtes du Rhône Villages, and wines from named villages. Recently 10 ha was added in Rasteau to replace a vineyard that was lost in Cairanne. The fourth generation of winemakers, Daniel took over the estate in 1987, but until 1999, he sold the grapes to the cooperative. A winery was built the following year. At 25-30 hl/ha, yields are significantly lower than the 45 hl/ha limit for the Côtes du Rhône.

Most of the cuvées are blends based on Grenache, with Syrah, Mourvèdre, Carignan, and other varieties in lesser proportions depending on the location, but there are some monovarietal wines. The Côtes du Rhône Le Cros is pure Syrah. The Cairanne L'Ancestrale du Puits and the Rasteau are almost pure (90%) Grenache. The Côtes du Rhône is a blend of Grenache, Carignan, and Mourvèdre, the Villages Vieilles Vignes is Grenache and Mourvèdre, and the Cuvée des Galets is GSM. The Cuvée 3 Cépages is equal parts of Grenache, Syrah, and Mourvèdre; it is partly harvested as a field blend (very late, when the Mourvèdre is ripe, so the Syrah and Grenache are extremely concentrated).

The top cuvées are matured in oak, with Le Cros the only cuvée to use barriques. The style is rich and powerful, often with alcohol levels pushing 15%, and the wines have been compared with Gigondas and Châteauneuf-du-Pape.

Domaine Brusset

70, Chemin de la Barque, 84290 Cairanne
(33) 04 90 65 81 56
Daniel & Laurent Brusset
domaine-brusset@wanadoo.fr
www.domainebrusset.fr
Côtes du Rhône Villages Cairanne
Gigondas, Les Hauts de Montmirail
87 ha; 250,000 bottles [map p. 81]

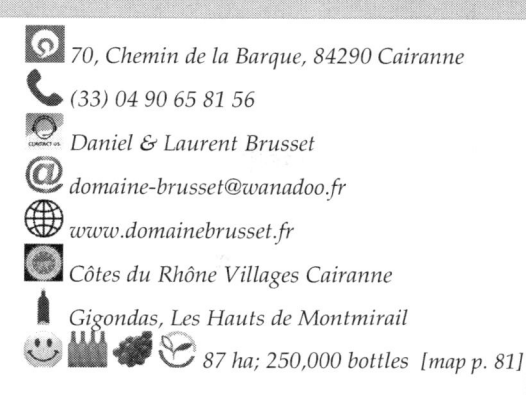

This family domain has its winery in Cairanne, where André Brusset started with 3 ha of vines and apricots when he returned from the second world war. Initially grapes were sold to the cooperative, and then André began to bottle himself. "He had the three colors (red, white, and rosé) so he could sell to restaurants," says his grandson, Laurent, recollecting a somewhat different era. Laurent's father, Daniel, took over with 5 ha and expanded the domain. Daniel has retired now, but still mans the tasting room in Cairanne. There is also a tasting room in Gigondas village.

More than half the vineyards (around 38 ha) are still in Cairanne, with Gigondas the next largest holding. "It was difficult to buy vineyards, but with the *crise*, it became easier. We are strictly an estate business, no negociant activity," says Laurent. In 1986, Daniel bought 18 ha on the Dentelles: it took twenty years to construct the vineyard, with 68 terraces. At one point the domain reached 90 ha, but since then has cut back a bit. Today there are vineyards in five appellations. The focus is on reds, but "we are planting more whites," Daniel says.

A major part of the range consists of entry-level wines, coming from Côtes du Rhône or Ventoux, sometimes with a touch of carbonic maceration to bring out fruitiness and make for immediate approachability. "We don't do the same vinification for Ventoux and Gigondas, they are different wines," says Daniel. The wines ferment in stainless steel or concrete, and age in stainless steel, with some wood used for Gigondas and some old Cairanne.

The style for the Crus tends towards supple fruits. "People think of Gigondas as a vin de garde with rustic tannins, but it can be more delicate and velvety. A new generation of vignerons like more delicate wines," says Laurent. Rasteau is light and elegant. There are three cuvées from Gigondas. Tradition Le Grand Montmirail shows more depth but less precision than Rasteau. Les Hauts de Montmirail shows the tautness that comes from the highest vineyards in the Dentelles, and has greater aging potential. A selection from the terraces, Les Secrets de Montmirail is the most refined.

Domaine Gourt de Mautens *

2001 Route de Cairanne, 84110 Rasteau
(33) 04 90 46 19 45
Jérôme Bressy
info@gourtdemautens.com
www.gourtdemautens.com
Rasteau
IGP Vaucluse
15 ha; 20,000 bottles [map p. 81]

It's ironic that Jérôme Bressy was one of the producers who helped Rasteau obtain promotion to a separate appellation, but has been forced by the rules of the new appellation to withdraw his wines. Committed to preserving the old varieties of the region, he planted Picardin to include in his white, and Vaccarèse, Counoise, Carignan, Cinsault, and Terret to include in the red. " I like to make all the grape varieties of the region, it's our history and identity," Jérôme says. "I have all the old varieties intermingled in the vineyard." The problem is not so much with the varieties themselves, but with the fact that their proportions exceed the permitted limits. (Rasteau allows up to 12% Picardin in white, and up to 15% in total for the indigenous black varieties; and Syrah and Mourvèdre must be at least 20%.) The Syndicat ruled that his wines should be excluded from 2012, but in response he labeled all his wines as IGP Vaucluse from 2010. "Declassifying everything is the only solution that allows me to continue my philosophy," Jérôme says.

The grapes from this family domain (with vines 30- to 100-years old) were sold to the cooperative until Jérôme took over in 1996, making wine in temporary space until the cave was constructed in 1998. All the vineyards are in Rasteau, with 12 ha red and 3 ha white, spread over seven terroirs that differ in soils and exposure, but are mostly calcareous. One cuvée is produced in each color. Aged in foudres, the white is lightly aromatic and moves in a savory direction as it ages. Showing the rich aromatics of Grenache (about 50% of the blend), the red is matured in a mix of concrete, foudres, and demi-muids for 24 to 36 months. Jérôme mentions Jacques Reynaud of Château Rayas and Henri Bonneau of Châteauneuf-du-Pape as his models. "Rasteau isn't yet a great appellation like Châteauneuf-du-Pape," he says, "it has fifty years of history with sweet wine, and the history of dry wine has just started." Expelling one of its top producers will not help.

Montirius

1536 Route de Sainte Edwige, 84260 Sarrians
(33) 04 90 65 38 28
Christine & Eric Saurel
contact@montirius.com
www.montirius.com
Côtes du Rhône
Vacqueyras, Garrigues

63 ha; 150,000 bottles   [map p. 80]

Montirius is the domain of the Saurel family, now in its fifth generation, under Christine and Eric since 1986. Their daughter Justine is taking over now. Christine and Eric have strong convictions and were among the first to adopt biodynamics. "When we started in 1986, we were in the cooperative, after we went biodynamic we tried hard to get the coop to do it, but it was too early for them," Christine says. A new winery was constructed in 2002 so that all production could be bottled on site.

Vineyards are spread over 35 separate plots, with 32 ha in Vacqueyras, 16 ha in Gigondas, and the rest in Côtes du Rhône and IGP. No wood is used for fermentation or aging, which is all in concrete tanks to emphasize purity of fruit; the Saurels describe their wines as "100% non boisé" (no wood). In Côtes du Rhône there are both blends of Grenache and Syrah, and monovarietals of each. Jardin Secret is 100% Grenache from 100-year-old vines, and comes from Sablet. Sérine is 100% Syrah and comes from Sarrians. The difference is like a comparison of the southern Rhône with the north, richness versus freshness.

Three red cuvées from Vacqueyras are all blends of Grenache and Syrah: Le Village comes from the youngest vines (less than 15-years old) and is 60% Grenache, Garrigues comes from the oldest vines (around 75-years) and is 70%, while Les Clos comes from a single parcel around the cellar and has 50% Grenache. You can't rank the cuvées by Grenache content, however, as Clos is the most concentrated and shows its Grenache most obviously. "We expected to use it for the Garrigues cuvée, but the taste is so different that we've made a separate cuvée," Christine says.

All the cuvées from Gigondas are 80% Grenache, 20% Mourvèdre. The young vines cuvée is La Tour; Terre des Aînés comes from 75-year-old vines, as does Confidential which is a parcel selection. The change to Mourvèdre as the second variety gives the wines more structure, and they generally need more time to start, and will age longer. Terre des Aînés is a real vin de garde; Confidential has great purity and concentration.

Domaine de La Mordorée ★

Chemin-des-Oliviers 30126 Tavel

(33) 04 66 50 00 75

Madeleine & Ambre Delorme.

info@domaine-mordoree.com

www.domaine-mordoree.com

Tavel

Châteauneuf-du-Pape, La Reine de Bois

Tavel, La Dame Rousse

50 ha; 220,000 bottles
[map p. 80]

This must be one of the more widely dispersed domains in the southern Rhône. Although based in Tavel, it has 38 different vineyard parcels in several different appellations. It was only in 1986 that Francis Delorme and his son Christophe decided to focus on winemaking and to expand their vineyards. Christophe's brother Fabrice joined in 1999, and Christophe is the winemaker today. Starting with 5 ha, they now have holdings in Lirac, Tavel, Châteauneuf-du-Pape, and Côtes du Rhône.

The wines are divided into two lines in most appellations, the introductory cuvée, La Dame Rousse, and the top cuvée, La Reine des Bois. In Châteauneuf-du-Pape there is a super cuvée, La Plume du Peintre, produced only in some vintages from hundred-year-old Grenache vines. Viticulture was lutte raisonnée because Christophe was worried about the high use of copper in organic cultivation, but with newer techniques reducing use of copper, the domain became organic in 2007. Everything is destemmed, and fermentation is at relatively high temperature to bring out structure.

The wines tend to be powerful and aromatic. The Châteauneuf cuvées are well regarded, but it's in Lirac and Tavel that the domain really makes its mark by producing wines well above the usual appellation level. The Tavel cuvées are complex blends (60% Grenache plus Cinsault, Syrah, Bourboulenc, Clairette, and Mourvèdre in La Dame Rousse); 48 hour cold maceration gives high color and strong aromatics.

Domaine de L'Oratoire Saint-Martin *

570 Route de Saint Roman de Malegarde, 84290 Cairanne

(33) 04 90 30 82 07

Frédéric & François Alary

falary@wanadoo.fr

www.oratoiresaintmartin.fr

Côtes du Rhône Villages Cairanne

25 ha; 100,000 bottles
[map p. 81]

Located on a road winding up into the hills from Cairanne, this is not a typical domain of the Côtes du Rhône on the plain. Vineyards are on steep slopes to the northeast of Cairanne, only a couple of hundred meters from to the hills of Rasteau, on pebbly soils with a high content of clay and active limestone. Production is 80% red. White varieties (half Marsanne) and Syrah are planted on slopes at Douyes (the coolest terroir) around 200 m altitude with northeasterly exposure; Grenache (60% of black plantings) and Mourvèdre (30%), are planted on the slopes at St. Martin with southerly exposure.

The Alary family has been making wine since 1692, and the vineyards have a good proportion of old vines. Yields are low, typically around 25 hl/ha (the oldest vines are not being replaced, even though yields are down to 15 hl/ha). Brothers Frédéric and François have been running the domain since 1984, with Frédéric making the wine and François managing the vineyards. The domain was constructed in the 1950s when Frédéric's grandfather started to bottle his own wines—the first in Cairanne to do so, says Frédéric proudly. Most of the vineyards are in the Côtes du Rhône Cairanne AOP, with a few in Côtes du Rhône. Each of the brothers owns 6 ha; the remaining vineyards are rented.

Three quarters of production is red, with two introductory-level cuvées from the Côtes du Rhône, and three cuvées from Cairanne: Réserve des Seigneurs is Grenache based, and matured in tank; Haut-Coustias is Mourvèdre, with Grenache and Syrah as the minor components, and is matured in foudres; and Les Douyes (formerly called Cuvée Prestige) is Grenache and Mourvèdre from hundred-year-old vines, matured in foudres for eighteen months. Mourvèdre is the favorite grape. "In hot years, its late development allows lower alcohol," says Frédéric. Looking to increase purity, the Alary's have become more noninterventionist, and have stopped punch-down or punchdown. The richness of the wines is often compared with Châteauneuf-du-Pape.

The tasting room is nominally open on a drop-in basis, but reception can be somewhat unfriendly when it is busy.

Domaine Rabasse Charavin *

Cuvée LAURE

La Font d'Estevenas, 84290 Cairanne
(33) 04 90 30 70 05
Laure Couturier
rabasse-charavin@orange.fr
www.rabasse-charavin.com
Côtes du Rhône Villages Cairanne
Cairanne, d'Estevenas
Cairanne, d'Estevenas

40 ha; 100,000 bottles   [map p. 81]

Edmond Rabasse purchased a small plot of land in 1890, and the estate took its present form when his granddaughter Jeanne married Abel Charavin in 1950. Their daughter Corinne took over in 1984, and her daughter Laure took over in 2014. The domain is located just outside the village of Cairanne. Vineyards run across Cairanne and Rasteau, all within 10 km of the domain, and have a high proportion of old vines. There are also vineyards in Violès, which are Côtes du Rhône. "We work by parcels, so there are many cuvées," Corinne says. In addition to the bottled wines, some of the cuvées are also available as bag-in-box.

The dozen cuvées break down into three white, a rosé, and about 9 reds. The whites are bottled under carbon dioxide to avoid oxidation, and are unusually elegant for the region. Côtes du Rhône Laure is Clairette and Roussanne, Cairanne is Clairette and Bourboulenc and a little more aromatic, and the Cairanne cuvée d'Estevenas comes from a tiny plot by the winery, and with a majority of Roussanne is the most refined.

All wines are aged in concrete to maintain purity of fruit. Vinification is the same for all the reds. The Côtes du Rhône Laure cuvée has 85% Grenache and 15% Cinsault, and can be a little on the tart side. In some years there is a pure varietal Syrah from a plot just south of Rasteau, which can be quite aromatic.

There are three red cuvées from Cairanne. The regular cuvée from the Cru is a GSM. No. 1 by Couturier has the same composition, but comes from parcels just outside the village that aren't in the Cru and so is labeled Cairanne CDR Villages. Cuvée d'Estevenas, which comes from old vines Grenache and Syrah on a south-facing plot at elevation on the slopes, makes by far the most sophisticated impression. The Rasteau is more savory than Cairanne, and the Abel Charavin Rasteau cuvée, which is old vines Grenache and Mourvèdre, is the most sophisticated of all.

Domaine de La Réméjeanne

La Réméjeanne, Cadignac-Nord, 30200 Sabran

(33) 04 66 89 44 51

Olivier& Rémy Klein

contact@remejeanne.com

www.remejeanne.com

Côtes du Rhône

Côtes du Rhône, Les Arbousiers

38 ha; 130,000 bottles

[map p. 80]

Located on the west side of the Rhône, approaching the foothills of the Cevennes, the domain is well away from the main plain of the Côtes du Rhône. Vineyards on the slopes facing east are Côtes du Rhône, while the warmer sites facing southeast are Côtes du Rhône Villages; altitudes range from 200 to 280m. The combination of altitude and exposure to the mistral gives the wine better freshness than usually found in Côtes du Rhône. Soils are calcareous, with clay and sandstone.

Réméjeanne was founded in 1960 when François Klein returned from Morocco and purchased 5 ha of vineyards. Grapes were sold to the cooperative, the vineyards were expanded, and then the domain was created when estate bottling started in 1975. It includes 2 ha of olive trees and 0.5 ha of figs as well as vines. Rémy Klein took over from his father in 1988, continued to expand the domain, and has been helped by his son Olivier since 2009.

There are about ten cuvées; all the reds are blends, varying from 80% Grenache to 80% Syrah. Winemaking is modern: grapes are destemmed, there is cold maceration, and after fermentation the wines are matured in cuve (except for the cuvées Les Eglantiers (mostly Syrah) and Les Prunelles (pure Bourbolenc), which go into demi muids). The white Côte du Rhône, Les Arbousiers, is a blend of the usual suspects (Viognier, Roussanne, Marsanne, Bourboulenc and Clairette). The style is generally straightforward.

Domaine Marcel Richaud

470 Route de Vaison La Romaine, 84290 Cairanne

(33) 04 90 30 85 25

Claire Richaud

marcel.richaud@wanadoo.fr

Côtes du Rhône Villages Cairanne

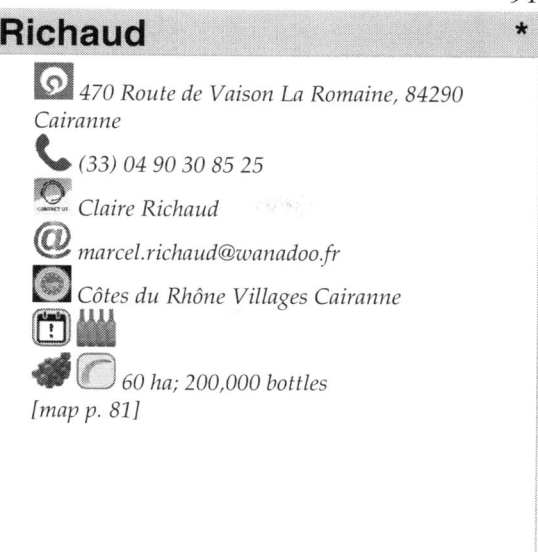

60 ha; 200,000 bottles
[map p. 81]

Marcel Richard inherited half of his vineyards and built up the domain by purchasing or renting other plots with different terroirs from those he had already. He took over the family estate in 1974, left the cooperative, and started estate bottling. His children Thomas and Claire are slowly taking over now. Most of the crop is vinified at the domain, but some grapes are sold off.

The range extends from Vin de France (all three colors) to Cairanne and Rasteau. The Vin de France red comes from young vines, 4-6 years old, and unusually for this level, includes 40% Mourvèdre, giving it more structure than you might expect. In Côtes du Rhône, Les Buisserons (the name refers to the bush-like pruning of the vines) is moistly Grenache, while Terre de Galets is a GSM with some Carignan, and is deeper and rounder. These are all aged in cuve.

The Cairanne Is also GSM with Carignan, and comes mostly from old vines near the village. It has a little oak exposure, and comes in two versions, with and without sulfur added at bottling (distinguished by a statement on the back label). With sulfur, the fruits are softer and blacker, without the wine is lighter and more elegant. The Rasteau is 60% Grenache and 40% Syrah, and the structure from the Syrah nicely matches the richness of the Grenache. It would be the recommended reference wine, but production is small, and it may be hard to find.

"The Vin de France is intended to drink right away, the Côtes du Rhône should keep for 3-4 years, the Cairanne for 5-6 years, and the Rasteau for 5-6 years. L'Ebrescade is the cuvée for grande garde," says Claire Richaud. L'Ebrescade has roughly equal amounts of Grenache, Syrah, and Mourvèdre, and comes from old vines in a plot at 300m above the village. It ages in wood. A step-up from the Cairanne, it has a lightness and elegance that is not common for the region. Another special cuvée, Les Estrambords is predominantly Mourvèdre with some Grenache and Syrah.

Marcel has been committed to natural wine ever since he started; he uses low sulfur and does not believe in over-extraction; perhaps for these reasons, after a disagreement with INAO he had trouble obtaining the agrément for the AOP, so some cuvées, including L'Ebrescade and Les Estrambords, were labeled simply as Vin de France. It's Cairanne's loss.

Domaine Le Sang des Cailloux *

4853 Route de Vacqueyras, 84260 Sarrians

(33) 04 90 65 88 64

Frédéric & Serge Férigoule

contact@sangdescailloux.com

www.sangdescailloux.com

Côtes du Rhône

Vacqueyras

18 ha; 60,000 bottles

[map p. 66]

The name of Sang des Cailloux means blood from the stones. The domain originated when a single large property owned by the Ricard brothers was divided between them in 1975. Serge Férigoule's ambition was to be a winemaker, and after qualifying in oenology at Montpellier, he took charge of the vineyards at the domain in 1979. He became a partner in the domain in 1982, and then took over when M. Ricard retired in 1990. A new cuverie was built in 2001. The wines became Vacqueyras AOC when Serge took over, as the appellation was created that year. Sang des Cailloux is now widely considered one of the leading estates of Vacqueyras.

The vineyards are located on the stony Plateau des Garrigues, underneath the Dentelles de Montmirail. The traditional red cuvée confusingly alternates its name each year to have the name of one of Serge's three daughters, Floureto, Doucinello, and Azalaïs: but it remains the same 70% Grenache and 20% Syrah with small amounts of Mourvèdre and Cinsault. It is matured for six months in foudres. Cuvée Lopy is three quarters Grenache (from 65-year-old vines), and one quarter Syrah (from 40-year-old vines). In some years there's a small production of another vieilles vignes cuvée, Oumage. The style is generally powerful. The single white cuvée is less than 10% of production and is a blend of six varieties. Serge is famous not only for his wine, but for his handlebar moustache; since 1999 he has shared the winemaking with his son Frédéric.

Domaine La Soumade *

1655, Route d'Orange, 84110 Rasteau

(33) 04 90 46 13 63

Frédéric Roméro

dom-lasoumade@hotmail.fr

www.domainelasoumade.fr

Rasteau

Rasteau

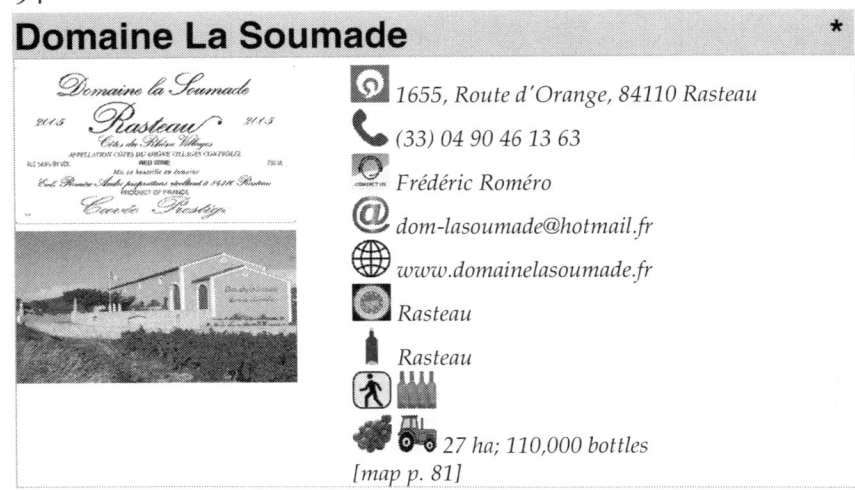

27 ha; 110,000 bottles
[map p. 81]

The Roméros have been involved in wine in the region for a long time, but the domain as such is relatively new, founded by André Roméro in 1979; he has been estate-bottling all the production since 1990. His son Frédéric has been involved since 1996. A new winery was constructed in 2002, when Stéphane Derenoncourt of Bordeaux was engaged as consulting oenologist. Domaine La Soumade is considered to be one of the leading producers in the appellation: the wines are a good demonstration of Rasteau's typicity vis à vis Gigondas and others. Almost all the vineyards are in Rasteau, with just 1 ha in Gigondas (close to the Dentelles). Soils are blue clay on limestone.

There are three cuvées from Rasteau: Cuvée Prestige (matured in a mix of foudres and cement) and Cuvée Confiance (matured in foudres) are both 70% Grenache, 20% Syrah, and 10% Mourvèdre; Fleur de Confiance comes from a specific vineyard parcel and is 90% Grenache and 10% Syrah, matured in demi-muids. Yields decline along this hierarchy from 35 hl/ha to 25 hl/ha to less than 18 hl/ha. The Gigondas is 70% Grenache to 30% Syrah. There are also two cuvées of Côtes du Rhône, one based on Grenache, but the other (Les Violettes) based on Syrah. There is no production of white wine, but a little Viognier is included in the reds. The range of appellation wines finishes with a rosé and VDN. The style is distinctly on the rich side: these are wines for people who like a really powerful style.

Maison Tardieu-Laurent ★

Les Grandes Bastides, Route de Cucuron, 84160 Loumarin

(33) 04 90 68 80 25

Bastien Tardieu

info@tardieu-laurent.com

www.tardieu-laurent.com

Côtes du Rhône Villages

St. Joseph

0 ha; 120,000 bottles

It's not easy to visit or gain information about the Tardieu Laurent negociant, which started as a collaboration between Dominique Laurent (from Burgundy, and noncommunicative if not secretive) and Michel Tardieu in 1994. Today it's run by Michel Tardieu, and has now become a family firm, with Bastien and Camille Tardieu joining their father. Michel is known for traveling constantly in the region to taste in each appellation. Since Dominique Laurent left, the concentration of new oak has been reduced. The firm is located in the southern Rhône and has been advised by well-known oenologue Philippe Cambie since 2000.

The wines are divided into three groups: Vieilles Vignes (always from vines more than fifty years old), Grandes Bastides (vieilles vignes from certain domains), and Vins à Façon, which is a special range developed for general distribution to the wine fairs. There are approximately fifty different cuvées from all over the Rhône, with the range headed by four Châteauneuf-du-Papes in the southern Rhône, and both red and white Hermitage in the northern Rhône. The Vieilles Vignes are regarded as points of reference in each appellation. They seem to me to offer unusual fruit purity, lifting the wines above the general level of the appellation, whichever it might be. The future is somewhat uncertain because supplies have been dwindling as more growers turn to bottling their own wines and there is increased competition for grapes with larger negociants.

Ventoux & Lubéron

Martinelle *

La Font Valet, 84190 Lafare

(33) 04 90 65 05 56

Corinna Faravel

corinna@martinelle.com

www.martinelle.com

Ventoux

12 ha; 40,000 bottles

[map p. 80]

It is not so easy to find producers to recommend in Ventoux, but Corinna Faravel (who is married to Thierry Faravel of Domaine la Bouissière in Gigondas) has been making waves with her winery, La Martinelle. Corinna started by making white wine in Germany's Nahe region, but became interested in the red wines of the Rhône. In 2001, she purchased vineyards at Martinelle, on the other side of the Dentelles from Gigondas and Vacqueyras. The first years were difficult, with torrential rains in 2002 and a hailstorm destroying the crop in 2003. So the first vintage was 2004, made in rented space: a cellar was constructed at Lafare in 2009.

The main production is Ventoux in red, white, and rosé, but there are also cuvées from Beaumes de Venise and Vin de France. A small vineyard in Beaumes de Venise was purchased in 2008, and has old vines of Grenache and some Syrah. Another source of old vines Grenache comes from a vineyard just to the south, and this is the basis of the Vin de France, which may also include grapes from the other vineyards; the exact blend varies with the year, and does not necessarily follow appellation rules.

All the red wines are driven by Grenache, typically with about three quarters in each blend. The Ventoux has Syrah, Mourvèdre, Carignan, and small amounts of other varieties, including some white grapes. The Beaumes de Venise red has a quarter Syrah, and Syrah is usually the other important grape in the Vin de France.

Château des Tourettes

Les Tourettes, 84400 Apt

(33) 04 90 74 27 34

Jean-Marie Guffens

info.verget@orange.fr

www.chateaudestourettes.com

Lubéron

IGP Vaucluse, Grande Trilogie

IGP Vaucluse, Plateau de l'Aigle

20 ha; 120,000 bottles

Château des Tourettes was the last addition to Jean-Marie Guffens's trio of properties, after the Guffens-Heynen domain and the Verget negociant in Mâcon. Guffens-Heynen dates from 1976, Verget from 1990, and Château des Tourettes was purchased in 1997. The domain was run down and required much replanting. It's in the Lubéron, but the varieties do not completely conform to appellation regulations, so the wines are labeled under the IGP Vaucluse. Grape varieties include Chardonnay, Roussanne, Marsanne, Viognier, Syrah, Grenache, and Cabernet.

Jean-Marie is never one to accept the traditional view, or as he might express it, to accept traditional limitations, and the aim here is to show freshness and precision in the wines, not the most common objective in the region. The red shows the aim of the house even more clearly than the whites: I would describe it as more like the northern than the southern Rhône. Grande Trilogie is the name for the blended cuvée, both red and white. Plateau de l'Aigle is a Chardonnay that shows as quite mainstream, with less evident aromatics than Grande Trilogie. There is also a range of whites from named varieties, including blends of Chardonnay-Viognier, Roussanne-Viognier and Marsanne-Roussanne. The style is modern with significant usage of new oak. I am not sure where one would place the wines in a blind tasting, but it would probably be in a more important appellation than the Lubéron.

Mini-Profiles of Important Estates

Châteauneuf du Pape

Domaine du Banneret

35 rue Porte Rouge, 84230 Châteauneuf-du-Pape
(33) 04 90 83 72 04
Jean-Claude & Audrey Vidal
domaine.banneret@gmail.com
www.domaine-banneret.fr

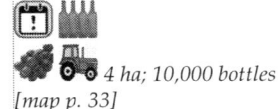

4 ha; 10,000 bottles
[map p. 33]

This tiny property is one of the most traditional producers in Châteauneuf, with only a single cuvée in each color. Vineyards fall into nine separate plots of old vines (with an average age of 70 years), which are replaced individually when necessary. All the grape varieties are grown, intermingled in each plot, and are cofermented. Winemaking follows old precepts, with no destemming, and long aging in old foudres (the winery describes them as "fûts anciens"). Jean-Claude Vidal was practicing as an architect but became a wine producer when he inherited the property in 1989; his traditional approach came from his mentor, Henri Bonneau, and is now continued by his daughter, Audrey.

Domaine de la Barroche

19, avenue des Bosquets, 84230 Châteauneuf-du-Pape
(33) 06 62 84 95 79
Julien Barrot
contact@domainelabarroche.com
www.domainelabarroche.com

15 ha; 30,000 bottles
[map p. 33]

Alexander Barrot founded the domain in 1703, and it took its present form when Christian Barrot took over in 1972 when it had only 3 ha. Most of the wine was sold in bulk to negociants. Estate bottling started when the next generation, Julien, took over in 2002. A new cellar was built in 2015 and fermentation now takes place in concrete eggs. Most of the varieties are grown (in the oldest plots varieties are intermingled), but the general blend has 55% Grenache, 18% Syrah, 12% Mourvèdre. Long maceration is followed by aging in demi-muids and foudres. The range was rationalized in 2012 and now consists of the general red Châteauneuf-du-Pape (Signature), a single foudre of monovarietal Grenache from 100-year-old vines (Pure), and an old vines cuvée (Liberty) that comes from vineyards in both Châteauneuf and Côtes du Rhône, and so is labeled as Vin de France. A small production of white was added in 2016.

Domaine Bosquet des Papes

18 Route d'Orange, 84230 Châteauneuf-du-Pape
(33) 04 90 83 72 33
Nicolas Boiron
contact@bosquetdespapes.com
www.bosquetdespapes.com

32 ha; 80,000 bottles
[map p. 33]

The estate was founded in 1860 when Emmanuel Boiron purchased vineyards in Châteauneuf. Maurice Boiron expanded the vineyards and established Bosquet des Papes as a domain in 1965. His son Nicolas joined in 1995, and expanded further in Châteauneuf and in Côtes du Rhône. Vineyards are particularly fragmented, with more than forty plots all over the appellation. There are four red cuvées in Châteauneuf, aged in foudres and demi-muids, with different amounts of new oak. Tradition is a GSM blend with 75% Grenache. Chante le Merle comes from 80-90-year-old vines, and is 80% Grenache with 10% each of Syrah and Mourvèdre, with new demi-muids included for aging; it's generally considered to be the top wine. La Jolie is 80% Grenache and 20% Mourvèdre, from 90-100-year old vines, and is aged in new foudres. Gloire de Mon Grand-Père is essentially a Grenache, from 60-70-year old vines. Philippe Cambie is consulting oenologue.

Clos des Brusquières

23 Route d'Orange, 84230 Châteauneuf-du-Pape
(33) 04 90 83 74 47
Claude Courtil
earl.courtil-thibaut@orange.fr
🛈 🍷
🍇 🍷 9 ha; 24,000 bottles
[map p. 33]

It is not surprising that this is one of the most traditional producers in Châteauneuf, because owner Claude Courtil, who took over in 1969 (when he was 17), learned winemaking from his godfather, Henri Bonneau (see profile). Today he runs the domain with his sons, David and Jérôme. The family has been making wine here since 1912; the winery is at the edge of the village, and most of the vineyards are in the Brusquières area to the north. The average age of the vines is more than 60 years. Until 1996 the production was sold to Mommessin and Guigal: today most of it is estate-bottled. There is only one (red) cuvée, which is driven by Grenache (more than 75%), with the rest mostly Syrah and Mourvèdre. The wine is aged in old foudres.

Domaine de la Charbonnière

26 Route de Courthézon, 84230 Châteauneuf-du-Pape
(33) 04 90 83 74 59
Caroline & Veronique Maret
contact@domainedelacharbonniere.com
www.domainedelacharbonniere.com
🛈 🍷
🍇 🍷 28 ha; 100,000 bottles
[map p. 32]

Eugène Maret bought the estate in 1912, and three generations later, Caroline and Veronique took over in 2014. Most the estate (20 ha) is in Châteauneuf, with the rest in Vacqueyras and Côtes du Rhône. Vacqueyras Tradition is a blend of 60% Grenache and 40% Syrah. About half of production is the Châteauneuf Tradition cuvée, a GSM with 70% Grenache, and 15% each of Syrah and Mourvèdre, which is a little more sophisticated. The real interest starts with the special cuvées from Châteauneuf. Mourre de Perdrix is a single vineyard wine; with the same GSM blend as Tradition, it moves in a more refined direction. With increasing elegance, the Vieilles Vignes is a selection from old vines of (mostly 90-year-old) Grenache and 5-10% Mourvèdre, and the Hautes Brusquières Cuvée Speciale (60% Grenache, 40% Syrah) comes from old vines on the plateau of Mont-Redon. Grenache is mostly aged in large oak vats, Syrah and Mourvèdre in barriques.

Domaine Charvin

Chemin de Maucoil, 84100 Orange
(33) 04 90 34 41 10
Laurent Charvin
domaine.charvin@free.fr
🛈 🍷
🍇 🍷 30 ha; 100,000 bottles
[map p. 32]

Founded in 1851, the property has been in the hands of the sixth generation since 1990. Laurent Charvin has significantly expanded the estate, which consisted of only 4 ha when he took over. In the north of the appellation, the estate is now about a third in Châteauneuf-du-Pape and two thirds in Côtes du Rhône. There is only a single cuvée from Châteauneuf, which is driven by Grenache from old vines. The Côtes du Rhône follows the Châteauneuf in style. Winemaking is traditional: no destemming and aging in concrete. The wines are vins de garde which need some time to come around.

Clos Saint Jean

Chemin du Moulin à Vent, 84230
Châteauneuf-du-Pape
(33) 04 90 83 58 00
Vincent Maurel
clos-st-jean@orange.fr
www.closstjean.fr

🚶 🏰

🍷 🍇 44 ha; 120,000 bottles
[map p. 33]

Founded in 1900 by the great great grandfather of brothers Vincent and Pascal Maurel, most of the vineyards of this relatively large domain are located on the famous plateau of La Crau, with the stony terroir of the galets. All but a hectare is planted with black varieties. All grapes are destemmed, maceration is traditionally long in concrete vats, and the varieties are treated differently during aging: Grenache is aged in concrete, but Mourvèdre and Syrah are aged in 1-2-year barrels. The major production is the domain Châteauneuf-du-Pape, 75% Grenache, 15% Syrah, and the rest of other varieties. Other cuvées are made in much smaller amounts. La Combe des Fous comes from 100-year-old vines, 60% Grenache. Deus ex Machina is a blend of 60% Grenache with 40% Mourvèdre. Sanctus Sanctorum is a 100% Grenache from 100-year-old vines, aged in demi-muids. Philippe Cambie is the consulting winemaker.

Domaine de Cristia

Fauburg Saint Georges 33,
Courthézon, 84350
(33) 04 90 70 89 15
contact@cristia.com
www.cristia.com

🍷 🍇

[map p. 32]

The domain was founded in 1942 with 2 ha of Grenache, and greatly expanded after 1963 by Alain Gangeon. His children Baptiste and Dominique took over the domain in 1999, moved to complete estate bottling, and continue to run the estate today. There are 13 ha in Châteauneuf-du-Pape in the immediate vicinity of the winery, around Courthézon in the eastern part of Châteauneuf-du-Pape. These have sandy-clay soils, but there's also a parcel on the galets, as well as vineyards in Côtes du Rhône and IGP beyond the limits of Châteauneuf-du-Pape. Wines are fermented in concrete. The appellation Châteauneuf-du-Pape is 85% Grenache and 15% Syrah, with Grenache aged in concrete and Syrah in barriques. The Vieilles Vignes is 100% Grenache from 95-year-old vines, aged in a mixture of barriques and demi-muids, with a third new oak. Cuvée Renaissance is 60% old vines Grenache and 40% Mourvèdre, aged in a similar mix. Côtes du Rhône and IGP age in concrete. In addition to the domain wines, there are also wines from elsewhere in the region under the negociant label of Cristia Collection.

Domaine Font de Michelle

14 Impasse des Vignerons, 84370
Bédarrides
(33) 04 90 33 00 22
Bertrand & Guillaume Gonnet
egonnet@terre-net.fr
www.font-de-michelle.com

🚶 🏰 🍷 🛢 🍇

48 ha; 210,000 bottles   [map p. 32]

The Gonnets produce wines under three labels: Font de Michelle (in Châteauneuf-du-Pape), Font du Vent (in Côtes du Rhône), and Gonnet Père et Fils (the negociant arm). The Gonnet family has been installed at the original domain, the Font de Michelle, since 1600; the buildings were constructed in 1880 by Jean-Etienne Gonnet, and the domain was established in 1950 by his grandson, Etienne Gonnet. The Châteauneuf vineyards include a major holding on the slope from Bédarrides to the La Crau plateau. La Font du Vent is a domain at Signargues, which they purchased in 2002; it

Domaine Giraud
19 Chemin le Bois de la Ville, 84230
Châteauneuf-du-Pape
(33) 04 90 83 73 49
Marie & François Giraud
contact@domainegiraud.fr
www.domainegiraud.fr
🚶 ⛉
🍇 🚜 35 ha; 70,000 bottles
[map p. 33]

Mas Saint-Louis
28, Avenue du Baron Le Roy, 84230
Châteauneuf-du-Pape
04 90 83 73 12
geniest-Châteauneuf@orange.fr
www.geniest-Châteauneuf.fr
🚶 ⛉
🚜 ⚙ 30 ha
[map p. 33]

101

produces red and rosé Côtes du Rhône, and some special cuvées from Signargues. Gonnet Père et Fils produces both Châteauneuf and Côtes du Rhône. Font de Michelle produces three red and two white cuvées. The main cuvée is 70% Grenache, 10% Syrah, 10% Mourvèdre, and 10% other varieties, aged in old foudres and barriques. In top years, Etienne Gonnet is a blend from 100-year-old Grenache with a little Syrah and Mourvèdre, and Elegance de Jeane is a 100% old vines Grenache. The style tends to be quite aromatic, becoming more subtle going up the hierarchy. The white is a blend, and in top years there is also a white Etienne Gonnet which is an equal blend of old vines Roussanne (aged in new oak) and Grenache Blanc. There's also a Vin de France under the Font de Michelle label.

The domain was created relatively recently when Pierre Giraud rented 4 ha of vineyards. The first vintage was bottled at the domain in 1981. Today the second generation, Marie and François, are in charge of vineyards dispersed among 64 parcels. The domain includes an 8 ha plot on the galets, which includes 100-year-old vines of Grenache. About a third of plantings are overall are Syrah, and this is reflected in the Tradition cuvée (60% Grenache and 35% Syrah). Les Gallimardes is 90% 100-year-old Grenache with 10% Syrah, while Les Grenache de Pierre is 100% old vines Grenache. The Grenache and Mourvèdre are aged in concrete, and Syrah is aged in barriques. Premices is a lighter cuvée from young vines Grenache. The Côtes du Rhône is also 100% Grenache, from 60-year-old vines on sandy terroir. Philippe Cambie is the consulting winemaker.

Mas Saint-Louis is the domain of the Geniest family, founded in 1909 by Jean-Louis Geniest, from a family of coopers, when he purchased the property in which the domain is still located in order to make wine from some parcels around the old Mas Saint-Louis that gave the domain its name. His grandson, also Jean-Louis, expanded the domain by buying more parcels until it consisted of a single block of 30 ha (located in the south part of the appellation). Today it is run by Jean Geniest's wife, Monique. Until 2011, the wine was sold to negociants; now there are 3 reds and 1 white wine bottled at the estate. The major red cuvée, Classique is intended to be consumed young, while Les Arpents des Contrebandiers has more structure; both are 80% Grenache with Mourvèdre, Syrah, and Counoise, and age in a mix of concrete vats and wood. The top cuvée is the Grande Réserve, a blend of 80% Grenache and 20% Mourvèdre, aged in demi-muids.

Domaine de Nalys

Route de Courthézon, 84230 Châteauneuf-du-Pape
(33) 04 90 83 72 52
Isabelle Ogier
contact@domainedenalys.com
www.domainedenalys.com

52 ha; 180,000 bottles
[map p. 32]

This old estate made its reputation after Dr. Philippe Dufays took over in 1955, when it became a pioneer for modernization in the appellation. The estate was broken up in 1976 when half was sold to an insurance company and the other half of the vineyards were dispersed. A somewhat uninteresting period followed. Guigal purchased the estate in 2017; winemaker Isabelle Ogier remains and it has to be seen what will change.

Ogier Cave des Papes

10 Avenue Louis Pasteur, 84232 Châteauneuf-du-Pape
(33) 04 90 39 32 32
caveau@ogier.fr
www.ogier.fr

94 ha; 6,000,000 bottles
[map p. 33]

Ogier is one of the largest negociants in the southern Rhône, and although it functions under its own name, it is now part of a larger group. Ogier et fils was founded in 1859 as a negociant, solely trading in wine, and then in 1948 became a négociant-éleveur also producing wine. When Ogier merged with Caves de Papes, the firm became known as Ogier Caves des Papes. In 1994 it became part of Vignobles JeanJean, and then when JeanJean merged with Laroche in Chablis, the holding company was renamed AdVini. Ogier purchased Clos l'Oratoire des Papes (see mini-profile) in 2000 and runs it as an independent domain. Under the name of Maison Ogier, they introduced a series of terroir-driven wines from Châteauneuf-du-Pape in 2011, with names like Galets Roules, Grès Rouge, Eclats Calcaires, to reflect the character of the soils. These are the top wines, but there is a wide range from appellations all over the southern Rhône.

Clos de L'Oratoire des Papes

10, avenue Louis Pasteur, 84230 Châteauneuf-du-Pape
(33) 04 90 39 32 41
Anne Cantineaux
acantineaux@ogier.fr
www.closdeloratoire.fr

25 ha; 50,000 bottles
[map p. 32]

This domain started out as a small vineyard of Syrah, given to the Amouroux family in 1880 as a wedding gift. It's been vinified under its present label since 1926. In 2000, Léonce Amouroux sold it to Maison Ogier (see mini-profile), and from 2006 other parcels were added to the domain. Grenache dominates (80%), with Syrah, Mourvèdre, and Cinsault. It is aged in foudres. There is also a small amount of white, made from equal amounts of Grenache Blanc, Clairette, and Roussanne, aged in new barriques. A new winery, at an old bastide in Courthézon, the Domaine de l'Etang Salé, was constructed for the 2015 vintage.

Domaine Pontifical

19 Avenue Saint Joseph, 84230 Châteauneuf-du-Pape
(33) 04 90 83 70 91
François Laget
francois.laget@wanadoo.fr

16 ha; 50,000 bottles
[map p. 33]

The domain was founded in 1883 and took its modern form when François Laget inherited it and renamed it as Domaine Pontifical in 1978. Vineyards are in thirty separate parcels, mostly in the western part of the appellation. The red cuvée is 75% Grenache and aged in old foudres; the white is 60% Grenache Blanc and aged in a mix of foudres and barriques. A Vieilles Vignes cuvée, Vignes d'Albert, from 90% Grenache and 10% Syrah, was introduced in 2007.

Domaine Raymond Usseglio

84 Chemin Monseigneur Jules Avril, 84230 Châteauneuf-du-Pape
(33) 04 90 83 71 85
Raymond Usseglio
info@domaine-usseglio.fr
www.domaine-usseglio.fr

35 ha; 60,000 bottles
[map p. 33]

Raymond Usseglio created a domain in his own name in 1963 when his brother Pierre took over the vineyards established by their father, Francis (see profile). Raymond's son, Stéphane, has been in charge since 2004. There are wines from both Châteauneuf and Côtes du Rhône. The classic Châteauneuf is an 80% Grenache blend from many terroirs, Les Claux has equal parts of Grenache, Syrah, and Mourvèdre from 50-year-old vines, and Imperial comes from a field blend of vines over 110 years of age, roughly 90% Grenache. Girard is exported exclusively to the United States and is a blend with 90% Grenache from 80-year-old vines. The white Les Claux is an equal blend of Grenache Blanc, Roussanne, and Clairette, and Roussanne Pur is monovarietal, barrel-fermented and aged in barriques.

Château de Vaudieu

501 Route de Courthézon, 84230 Châteauneuf-du-Pape
(33) 04 90 83 70 31
Laurent Bréchet
christophe.schurdevin@famillebrechet.com
www.famillebrechet.fr

70 ha; 190,000 bottles
[map p. 32]

Vaudieu is a grand château built in 1767 and had a high reputation for its wines in the nineteenth century. After falling into disrepair, it was bought in 1955 by Gabriel Meffre, who was to become a large negociant (see mini-profile). The estate is in effect a family domain, as it was inherited by Gabriel's daughter, Sylvette, and her husband Michel Brechet (together with Domaine des Bosquets in Gigondas). Sylvette's son Laurent is in charge of the domain today. The domain red is three quarters Grenache (aged in vat) and a quarter Syrah (aged in barriques). Val de Dieu is a cuvée with a quarter Mourvèdre. Les Temps Rouge is a selection of almost pure Grenache from terroir of galets. Avenue Rouge is a 100% Grenache selected from sandier terroirs. Aside from the domain red, all the cuvées are aged in demi-muids. The white is a blend of three quarters Grenache Blanc and a quarter Roussanne, Clos du Belvédère is 100% Grenache Blanc. The domain also produces Lirac and Côtes de Provence. Philippe Cambie is the consulting winemaker.

Gigondas-Vacqueyras-Beaumes de Venise

Domaine des Bosquets

2 Chemin des Bosquets, 84190
Gigondas
(33) 04 90 65 80 45
Julien Brechet
secretariat@domainedesbosquets.com
www.domainedesbosquets.com

26 ha; 20,000 bottles
[map p. 66]

Gabriel Meffre bought this domain in 1962, and it was inherited by his daughter Sylvette, together with Château de Vaudieu (see mini-profile). Sylvette's son Julien has been in charge since 2006. The cellar has been renovated and there is a dedicated tasting room. The Gigondas is a blend with 75% Grenache, 15% Syrah, and 5% Mourvèdre, partly aged in cuve and partly in barriques. Le Plateau is based on old vines Mourvèdre, with Grenache and Syrah, and ages in demi-muids and barriques. La lieu-dit comes from a 1 ha parcel of Grenache, and La Colline is 100% Grenache from high altitude plots, both aged in demi-muids. There is also a rosé and Côtes du Rhône Blanc.

Domaine des Florets

1467 Route des Florets, 84190
Gigondas
(33) 04 90 40 47 51
Jérôme Boudier
scea-domainedesflorets@orange.fr
www.domainedesflorets.com

8 ha
[map p. 66]

Located at the foot of the Dentelles de Montmirail, the domain has vineyards at up to 500m elevation. Myriam and Jérôme Boudier bought the property and have been making wine since 2007. The domain wine is 80% Grenache, 15% Syrah, and 5% Mourvèdre. Grapes are destemmed and the wine ages in cuve. The 3S red comes from vines with an average age of 50 years, and is 80% Grenache with 20% Syrah; grapes are destemmed and there is short maceration. The white comes from old vines of 70% Grenache Blanc and 30% Clairette.

Domaine de Font-Sane

446, Chemin du Grame, 84190,
Gigondas, 84190
(33) 04 90 65 86 36
Véronique Cunty
domaine@font-sane.com
www.font-sane.com

16 ha; 45,000 bottles
[map p. 66]

This family domain dates from 1860 and today is run by Veronique and Bernard Cunty-Peysson, and their son Romain. Located just outside the village of Gigondas, the domain has 12 ha in Gigondas and 4 ha in Ventoux. There are two cuvées from Gigondas: the Tradition cuvée is 72% Grenache and 23% Syrah with a little Mourvèdre and Cinsault;, the Terrasses des Dentelles comes from a 1.5 ha plot on the slopes of the Dentelles, and is GSM. Both age in wood The Ventoux is split between red from 60-year-old vines of Grenache and Syah, and a rosé.

Domaine les Goubert

235 Chemin des Jardinières, 84190
Gigondas
(33) 04 90 65 86 38
Mireille & Jean-Pierre Cartier
jpcartier@lesgoubert.fr
www.lesgoubert.fr

This old family domain has been in the Goubert family for generations; Jean-Pierre Cartier, who took over in the 1970s, is the son of Augusta Goubert. He is considered a pioneer of modernism in Gigondas: grapes are destemmed, there is cold maceration to increase color in the wine, and new oak is used in aging. The Gigondas Classique is the most traditional cuvée; a blend of the usual varieties, it ages in a mix of concrete and old oak. Cuvée Florence is a blend of Grenache and Syrah and

🚜 27 ha; 70,000 bottles
[map p. 66]

ages in barriques, with 70% new oak. Besides Gigondas, the range is quite extensive, with a red Beaumes de Venise, a Sablet Villages Côtes du Rhône, and a Côtes du Rhône in reds, with whites from Sablet and the Côtes du Rhône, and a Viognier monovarietal. Jean-Pierre's daughter, Florence, who is taking over, introduced a rosé, Rosé de Flo.

Domaine du Grapillon d'Or

617 Route des Princes d'Orange,
84190 Gigondas
(33) 04 90 65 86 37
Céline Chauvet
c.chauvet@domainedugrapillondor.com
www.domainedugrapillondor.com

19 ha; 80,000 bottles
[map p. 66]

Chauvets have been making wine in Gigondas since 1630, and the family domain was created in 1806 (prominently announced on the label). Bernard Chauvet has been in charge since the late 1970s, and his daughter Céline officially took over in 2012. Vineyards vary from the valley to the slopes with a variety of terroirs. The domain cuvée has 80% Grenache and 20% Syrah, and ages in foudres. Excellence is a selection from old vines, 60% Grenache and 40% Syrah, and ages in cuve. The Vacqueyras is also a Grenache-Syrah blend; an IGP Vaucluse is a blend of Merlot and Caladoc from vineyards close to Gigondas.

Clos du Joncuas

700 Route de Carpentras, 84190 Gigondas
(33) 04 90 65 86 86
Fernand Chastan
contact@closdujoncuas.fr
www.closdujoncuas.fr

29 ha
[map p. 66]

Founded in 1920 by Pierre Auguste Chastan, and run today by third generation of sisters Dany and Carole Chastan, Clos Joncuas is considered a traditional producer in Gigondas. Fermentation uses whole clusters, maceration is extended, and aging is in old foudres. The Gigondas (red and rosé) comes from vineyards on the classic Trias soils on the slopes of the Dentelles. Cuvée Esprit de Grenache comes from the oldest vines, 60-year-old Grenache. In addition to 11 ha in Gigondas, there are 6 ha in Vacqueyras and 13 ha in Séguret (producing red and white Côtes du Rhône). The domain is a pillar of the organic movement as it has been organic since its establishment.

Maison Gabriel Meffre

2 Le Village, Route des Princes d'Orange, 84190 Gigondas
(33) 04 90 12 30 21
Jasper van Berkel
gabriel-meffre@meffre.com
www.gabriel-meffre.fr

2,000,000 bottles
[map p. 66]

Gabriel Meffre came from a winemaking family, but started buying vineyards independently in 1936, and from the 1950s built up the negociant that bears his name. He also acquired several domains including Château de Vaudieu in Châteauneuf (see mini-profile) and Domaine des Bosquets in Gigondas (see mini-profile). When he died in 1987, he owned 900 ha of vineyards. His various domains were distributed among his children, Sylvette, Laurent, Jacques, and Christian, who provide a major source for the firm of Gabriel Meffre today, although none of them work for it. Gabriel Meffre became a public company in 1998, and in 2009 Jean-Claude Boisset of Burgundy acquired control. In Gigondas, where Meffre is based, half of production comes from estate grapes and half from purchased grapes; Laurus is the signature wine. Most of the production is IGP, including the major brand, Fat Bastard. In addition to the negociant activity, Gabriel Meffre owns Domaine de Longue Toque (purchased in 1999 with vineyards in Gigondas, Vacqueyras, and Côtes du Rhône). Gabriel Meffre wines are made in a large modern facility, just across the road from the Longue Tongue domain, where the tasting room is located.

Domaine de la Monardière
930 Chemin des Abreuvoirs, 84190 Vacqueyras
(33) 04 90 65 87 20
Damien Vache
info@monardiere.fr
www.monardiere.fr

22 ha; 80,000 bottles
[map p. 66]

Martine and Christian Vache took over the family estate in 1987, replanted many vineyards, constructed a new winery, and created their domain. Damien took over from his parents in 2014. Most of the vineyards are in Vacqueyras, with 4 ha in the IGP Vaucluse. All three colors come from Vacqueyras. There are three red cuvées: Les Calades (70% Grenache, 20% Syrah, 10% Cinsault aged in cuve) from sandier terroirs, Les 2 Monardes (70% Grenache, 30% Syrah aged in a mix of cuve and barriques) from slightly older vines on rockier soils, and the Vieilles Vignes from 60-year-old vines (a classic GSM with 60% Grenache, 20% Syrah, and 20% Mourvèdre aged in demi muids). The white is 50% Roussanne, 30% Grenache Blanc, and 20% Viognier and ages in demi muids. The rosé is an assemblage between saignée and direct pressing.

Domaine d'Ouréa
470 Chemin de Fontbonnne, 84190, Vacqueyras
(33) 06 76 71 32 44
Adrien Roustan
info@domainedourea.fr
www.domainedourea.fr

20 ha; 120,000 bottles
[map p. 66]

Adrian Roustan founded this new domain in 2010 when he graduated from oenology school in Burgundy. It's really off the beaten track, way out in the middle of the vineyards in a spot the GPS cannot find. "The vineyards come from my grandfather, who made wine but sold it to the negociants," Adrien says. They are all around, but not all in AOP. The major holding is 11 ha in Vacqueyras, with another 4 ha in Gigondas and 5 ha in Vin de France. There is one cuvée from each appellation, and a Côtes du Rhône for lots that are declassified from young vines in Vacqueyras. The Vacqueyras is 60% Grenache and the Gigondas is 80% Grenache. There is also a wine from the Vaucluse, Tire Bouchon, but it is labeled as Vin de France because it contains two old but unauthorized varieties, Oeillade and Aramon. Destemming depends on vintage; wines ferment in stainless steel, and age in concrete. Going up the range, the wines become more fragrant, more elegant, with increasing sense of precision, yet all have an attractive smoothness.

Domaine Raspail-Ay

737 Route des Princes d'Orange,
84190 Gigondas
(33) 04 90 65 83 01
Anne-Sophie Ay
raspail.ay@orange.fr
gigondas-vin.com

19 ha; 60,000 bottles
[map p. 66]

This is a famous old name in Gigondas, going back to 1854. Dominique Ay, who is the fifth generation, runs this domain, which represents about half of the original Raspail holdings (which were divided in the family). Located close to the village, the vineyard consists of a single block around the winery. Production is 95% red, the rest being a little rosé. The Gigondas is a GSM blend of 70-80% Grenache, 15-20% Syrah, and 5-10% Mourvèdre. The approach is traditional: grapes are harvested manually and given a long fermentation with indigenous yeasts; the Grenache is racked into old foudres, and kept for 18-24 months before being assembled with the Syrah and Mourvèdre, which have been matured in old barriques. The wine is rich in traditional style, a very solid representation of the appellation.

Mas des Restanques

713 Route de Carpentras, 84190
Gigondas
(33) 04 90 65 80 87
Jean-Luc & Josiane Faraud
masdesrestanques@hotmail.fr
www.masdesrestanques.com

12 ha; 18,000 bottles
[map p. 66]

The Farauds have vineyards in Gigondas and Vacqueyras from each side of the family; from 1995 to 2006 grapes went to the cooperative; then in 2007 they left the cooperative, created their own domain, changed to organic viticulture, and constructed a cave. The Gigondas and Vacqueyras are both 70% Grenache, but the Gigondas also has 30% Syrah while the Vacqueyras has 15% each of Syrah and Mourvèdre.

Domaine Saint Gayan

Domaine Saint Gayan, 84190
Gigondas
(33) 04 90 65 86 33
Meffre Jean-Pierre
contact@saintgayan.fr
www.saintgayan.com

38 ha
[map p. 66]

Located on the plain just below Gigondas, the domain is on the site of a Roman villa. Pierre Goubert bought the property in 1709, and it has remained in the hands of the same family ever since. Roger Meffre started estate bottling in 1956. His son Jean Pierre took over in 1980 and expanded the domain, partly by purchases, and partly with vineyards in Sablet and Rasteau inherited by his wife, Martine. Their son-in-law, Christian-Yves Carré de Lusançay, joined him in 2007. Almost half the vineyards are in Gigondas, with most of the rest in Côtes du Rhône, and smaller holdings elsewhere, making an unusually wide range of wines for a family domain. Côtes du Rhône, Rasteau, Gigondas, and Châteauneuf-du-Pape (from a parcel of less than a hectare acquired in 1987)are all GSM; Sablet is the one white wine. Vinification is traditional, with little destemming, and long fermentation. Côtes du Rhône and Rasteau age in concrete vat, Gigondas and Châteauneuf-du-Pape in oak (mostly demi-muids).

Domaine les Semelles de Vent

Chemin de Caveau, Quartier Les
Cinq Oliviers, 84190 Vacqueyras
(33) 06 75 74 62 34
Christophe Galon
galon.christophe@wanadoo.fr

[!] 🏭

🍇 🚜 12 ha
[map p. 66]

The domaine is located in Vacqueyras, but also has vineyards in Gigondas and a quarter hectare in Châteauneuf-du-Pape. Christophe Galon has been growing grapes at the family domain for 25 years, but only left the cooperative to start estate bottling in 2009. The domain has a lot of old vines, more than 60-years old for Grenache, and more than 40 years for Syrah and Mourvèdre. Vinification is traditional, with fermentation in concrete tanks followed by aging in old oak. There's a clear progress going up the appellations: Vacqueyras Seduction is a touch rustic, the Vieilles Vignes Vacqueyras is more structured and still quite sturdy (although it has more Grenache), the Gigondas is more aromatic and shows greater sophistication, and the Châteauneuf is structured and less evidently fruity, unusually coming from 100% Mourvèdre. Christopher designs the labels himself, changing them each year for a new photograph or drawing.

Côtes du Rhône, Lirac, and Tavel

Domaine Alary

1345 Route de Vaison, La Font d'
Estevenas, 84290 Cairanne
(33) 04 90 3O 82 32
Denis Alary
alary.denis@wanadoo.fr
www.domaine-alary.fr

🚶 🏭

🍇 🍇 30 ha; 100,000 bottles
[map p. 81]

The tasting room has a genealogical tree tracing ten generations of the Alary family in Cairanne back to 1692. The domain is entirely within Cairanne, but the variety of terroirs makes for a wide range of wines, from Cairanne, Côtes du Rhône, and IGP d'Orange. The reds are based on combinations of Grenache with other varieties, extending to some international varieties for the IGP. Whites are dominated by Roussanne and Clairette, with their aromatic southern character emphasized by fermentation at low temperature. In fact, both reds and whites have pronounced aromatic character.

Domaine de l'Amauve

197 Chemin du Jas, 84110 Séguret
(33) 06 10 71 26 72
Christian Voeux
contact@domainedelamauve.fr
www.domainedelamauve.fr/

[!] 🏭

🍇 🍇 11 ha; 40,000 bottles
[map p. 81]

Christian Voeux makes the wine at Château La Nerthe, one of the grand old properties of Châteauneuf-du-Pape (see profile). Since 2005, he has also run his family estate, created by the marriage of his parents in 1952. Estate bottling started when Christian took over. Located in Séguret, the domain has old vines on a pebbly, sandy terroir, divided in to 23 parcels, with 9 ha in Séguret and the rest in IGP. Côtes du Rhône Village Séguret comes in both red and white—unusually for the appellation, the white is something of a specialty here. The white La Daurèle comes from calcareous soils; faintly perfumed, it increases in intensity on the palate. "I always look for freshness and natural acidity to safeguard the fruit," Christian says. There are several red cuvées, generally three quarters Grenache with the rest exclusively Syrah or Syrah plus other local varieties. The top wine is La Réserve. The style is spicy, smooth, and elegant. In addition to the Côtes du Rhône, there's also some IGP de Vaucluse.

Domaine des Amouriers

5801 Route de la Garrigue de
L'étang 84260 Sarrians
(33) 04 90 65 83 22
Igor Chudzikiewicz
domaine@amouriers.com
www.amouriers.com

🚶 🏭
🍇 🍾 30 ha; 80,000 bottles
[map p. 66]

The name of the domain refers to the many mulberry trees (mûriers) on the property (amourier is local dialect for mûrier). The domain was established in 1928, but it was not until 1950 that Jocelyn Chudzikewicz developed it. His son Igor runs the domain today. Located between Vacqueyras and Sarrians, on the plateau of the garrigue (shrubs), it has vineyards in both villages and also the IGP de Vaucluse. The entry-level wine is the IGP de Vaucluse Suzanne, a blend of many local varieties and Merlot; there is also a white. Les Hautes Terrasses is a 100% Syrah from IGP Méditerranée, aged in demi-muids. There are three red cuvées from Vacqueyras, all GSMs. Signature is aged in concrete, Les Genestes comes from older vines and is also aged in concrete, and Les Truffières comes from old vines on the best terroirs, and is aged in demi-muids. There's also a rosé; recently a white Vacqueyras has been added.

Château d'Aqueria

Route de Roquemaure, 30126 Tavel
(33) 04 66 50 04 56
Vincent de Bez
contact@aqueria.com
www.aqueria.com

📧 🏭
🍇 🍷 68 ha; 380,000 bottles
[map p. 80]

One of the most important estates in Tavel and Lirac, with the unique property of having all its vineyards in one large holding within the estate of 98 ha, the domain takes its name from Joseph d'Aqueria, who bought the property in 1595. The splendid château was built in the eighteenth century. The domain passed through several proprietors until Jean Olivier family purchased it in 1919; his grandchildren Vincent and Bruno de Vez are in charge today. The center of the domain is divided between the Tavel and Lirac appellations, with vineyards to the west and east falling into Côtes du Rhône.

Château Beauchêne

Chemin de Beauchene, 84420 Piolenc
(33) 04 90 51 75 87
Michel Bernard
info@chateaubeauchene.com
chateaubeauchene.fr

🚶 🏭
🍇 🍾 70 ha; 350,000 bottles
[map p. 80]

The Bernard family were farmers in the area who bought their first vineyards in 1794 at the sale of property confiscated in the French Revolution. Michel and Dominique Bernard took over the estate in 1971, and in 1986 they acquired the château, which is now the winery. Their daughter Amandine joined the domain in 2004. This is a large producer, with most of the vineyards in the Côtes du Rhône, and 8 ha in Châteauneuf-du-Pape. The Côtes du Rhône is a good example of the modern style of the appellation; the Villages has just a little more depth. The Premier Terroir cuvée comes from plots near Châteauneuf-du-Pape and has more structure. The cuvées from Châteauneuf-du-Pape are distinguished by age of the vines: Vignobles da la Serrière from 20-year-old vines, Grande Réserve from older vines, and Hommage à Odette Bernard from 100-year-old vines. The Côtes du Rhône and Serrière are aged in stainless steel, the top cuvées in barriques. The Côtes du Rhône shows immediate fruits, very much what the appellation should be, and the Villages has more depth, but is still quite fruit-forward. Vignoble de la Serrière from Châteauneuf comes from young vines and is aged in steel; Grande Réserve comes from older vines, and has the smoothness of oak-aging. Hommage à Odette Bernard is the most refined Châteauneuf-du-Pape, smooth and silky.

Domaine Cécile Chassagne

3bis Route de Vaison 84110, Sablet
(33) 04 86 38 24 70
Cécile Chassagne
camassot.chassagne@wanadoo.fr
www.gigondas-vin.com

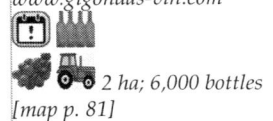

2 ha; 6,000 bottles
[map p. 81]

Jean-Claude Chassagne owned Domaine Camassot, with vines in the Côtes du Rhône and Gigondas. The vineyard in Gigondas was a small plot he planted in 1974, with 80% Grenache and 10% each of Syrah and Mourvèdre, at around 300m up the Dentelles de Montmirail. When he retired in 1998, he sold most of his vineyards, and his daughter Cécile created her domain with the plot in Gigondas. There is no destemming, fermentation takes place in open wooden vats, and the wine is aged briefly in new oak. Cécile has an artistic background and also paints; she has exhibited at the Maison des Vins in Sablet.

Domaine de la Charité

Chemin Issarts 5, 30650 Saze
(33) 06 07 60 83 41
Christophe Coste
contact@domainecharite.com
www.christophecoste.com

45 ha

Domaine de la Charité is in Saze, immediately to the west of Avignon. When it was founded in 1970, it had 5 ha, and grapes were sold to the cooperative until estate bottling started in 1974. Christophe Coste took over from his father in 1998, and has been expanding the estate, which is located in the Côtes du Rhône Village of Signargues; Christophe is president of the local Syndicat. Côtes du Rhône is the main production, with the major cuvée coming from 60% Grenache, 30% Syrah, and 10% Carignan. There are several monovarietal wines: Dame Noire is Mourvèdre (aged in barriques and foudres), Les Ombres (made since 2004) is Syrah aged in new barriques, and the white Dame Blanche is Viognier. Châteauneuf-du-Pape comes from a 1 ha plot of old vines Grenache that Christophe purchased in 2008. Vinification is quite innovative. There's a sorting machine that works according to sugar level, so riper grapes can be fermented separately, and fermentation takes place in horizontal steel tanks that rotate to mix the skins and juice. All the wines have a tightly structured impression; Les Ombres is silky and smooth, and Dame Noir has the monotonic intensity of Mourvèdre. The Châteauneuf is a powerful wine, showing its structure in cool years, and the aromatics of Grenache overpower the structure in warm years.

Domaine Coteaux Travers

15 route de la Cave, 84110 Rasteau
(33) 04 90 46 13 69
Marine & Paul Charavin
coteaux-des-travers@rasteau.fr
www.coteaux-des-travers.com

14 ha; 55,000 bottles
[map p. 81]

The name reflects the fact that vineyards are split between Rasteau (10 ha) and Cairanne (4 ha). The domain has been in the Charavin family since it was founded in 1920. Robert started estate bottling in 1976, and his children Marine and Paul took over in 2017. Plantings are mostly black, all the classic GSM trio. There are both red and white cuvées in Côtes du Rhône and Côtes du Rhône Villages. The Cairanne red is a blend from vineyards spread across the domain. From Rasteau in dry reds there are Les Travès (70% Grenache, 30% Syrah), La Mondonna (70% Grenache, 20% Syrah, 10% Mourvèdre), and Paul (made only in top years using only a few barrels). There's a move here towards more individual cuvées, with Lou Montel introduced in 2015 from a specific plot of old vines Grenache and Carignan. (In 2017 there was insufficient crop so the grapes went into La Mondonna.) From Rasteau there is also there is a series of sweet wines, with all the varieties of Vin Doux Naturel, all 100% Grenache.

Domaine des Escaravailles

111 Combe de l'Eoune, 84110 Rasteau
(33) 04 90 46 14 20
Gilles Ferran
domaine.escaravailles@wanadoo.fr
www.domaine-escaravailles.com

65 ha; 170,000 bottles
[map p. 81]

This family domain has been run since 1999 by Gilles Ferran, who is the grandson of Jean-Louis Ferran, who founded it in 1953. Two thirds of the vineyards are in Rasteau, with the rest in Cairanne and Roaix. The policy here is to harvest late for maximum ripeness. The white Cairanne has a powerful, aromatic style. The red cuvées come from the individual villages: Cairanne and Rasteau are Grenache with 20% Syrah (and 10% Carignan in Cairanne), aged in concrete or stainless steel. Roaix is 100% Syrah aged in barriques. There are also white Côtes du Rhône and Vin de France, and a small production of VDN (fortified sweet) from Rasteau. Philippe Cambie assists.

Domaine des Ondines

Quartier Garrigues Sud, 84260 Sarrians
(33) 04 90 65 86 45
Jérémy Onde
jeremy.ondines@wanadoo.fr
www.domaine-les-ondines.net

57 ha
[map p. 66]

The family has grown grapes for generations, and when Jérémy Onde took over in 2003, it included 18 ha of vineyards but the grapes were sold off. Jérémy built a cellar, and started bottling wine. Production has expanded considerably since then, the cellar was expanded in 2012, and then areas that grew other crops were replanted to vines. Half the vineyards are in Vacqueyras, with the rest in Côtes du Rhône and IGP, and a tiny plot in Beaumes de Venise. Vacqueyras comes in both red and white, Côtes du Rhône Village Plan de Dieu is red, and there is a white Côtes du Rhône.

Domaine de Piaugier

3 Route de Gigondas, 84110 Sablet
(33) 04 90 46 96 49
Jean-Marc Autran
info@domainedepiaugier.com
domainedepiaugier.com

30 ha; 150,000 bottles
[map p. 81]

The domain is located in Sable, where it has 12 ha, and also has vineyards in the Côtes du Rhône (14 ha) and Gigondas (4 ha). Now in its fourth generation, the domain is located in the cellars built by Jean-Marc Autran's grandfather in 1947 when he started to bottle the estate wines. Jean-Marc took over in 1984 and expanded the cellars in 1995. Some monovarietal wines come from the Côtes du Rhône; Rêve de Marine and the Réserve de Maude (from older vines) are Syrah, aged in barriques, while Ténébi is an unusual 100% Counoise. The Sablet is a Grenache-Syrah blend, the Sablet Les Briguières is Grenache and Mourvèdre, and the Gigondas is GSM. Wines are mostly aged in old barriques.

Domaine Rouvre Saint-Léger

Ferme de la Rouveyrolle, Route de Saint Laurent des Arbres, 30290 Laudun
(33) 06 17 33 80 26
Adrien Borrelly & Didier Dumont
contact@rouvresaintleger.com
www.rouvresaintleger.com

1 ha; 5,000 bottles
[map p. 80]

This tiny domain is a partnership between Adrien Borrelly, whose family owns the 60 ha Ferme de la Rouveyrolle, and Didier Dumont, an Italian who has been restoring a sixteenth century property at Laudun. They are making wine from a hectare of the Borelly family vineyards, with Philippe Cambie as consulting oenologue. The wines are Côtes du Rhône Village Laudun; there is equal production of red and white. The red is 60% Grenache and 40% Syrah; the white is Viognier with a little Roussanne. Both are partly aged in barriques.

Château Saint Roch

Chemin de Lirac, 30150 Roquemaure
(33) 09 67 13 82 59
Eve Brunel
eve.brunel@chateau-saint-roch.com
www.gardine.com/en/chateau-saint-roch-estate

40 ha; 200,000 bottles

One of the most important domains in Lirac, the property was bought in 1998 by the Brunels of Château La Gardine (see profile), and the wine is made by Eve Brunel at the cellars in Lirac. The vineyards are divided into 34 ha of red, planted with GSM, and 6 ha of white, planted with a mix of all the local varieties. The white Lirac is fermented in stainless steel with no MLF. It's mostly Clairette and Grenache Blanc, but has some Viognier, which gives it quite a perfumed impression. Confidentielle is 100% 90-year-old Clairette, fermented and aged in new oak. It's quite oaky when young. The reds tend to be rather powerful, in an oxidative style tending to show notes of prunes. The estate wine is a GSM blend, with 30% aged in 2-year barrels, the rest in cuve. Confidentielle comes from three plots of old vines, 55-year old, 75-year-old Mourvèdre, and 50-year-old. It's fermented in concrete, then MLF is finished off, and it ages, in new oak. "This is quite a modern style of Lirac," says marking manager Alban de Gérin. Palmes comes from 75-year-old Grenache, fermented and aged in concrete, and really plays on the fruits of Grenache, but shows less flavor variety than Confidentielle.

Domaine Sainte-Anne
Les Cellettes, 30200 Saint Gervais
(33) 04 66 82 77 41
Jean Steinmaier
domaine.ste.anne@orange.fr

🚶 ⛁

🍇 🚜 *35 ha; 100,000 bottles*
[map p. 80]

The Steinmaier family came from Vienna to Burgundy in the 1930s, and then in 1965 Guy Steinmaier purchased a vineyard in Saint-Gervais, which he extended 1973. His sons Alain and Jean took over in the 1980s. Wines are Grenache-based, with the Côtes du Rhône also including Syrah and Cinsault, the Côtes du Rhône Village comprising a blend of 70% Grenache and 30% Syrah, and the cuvée Notre-Dame being a GSM blend. Les Rouvières is an unusual blend based on 70% Mourvèdre, with 15% each of Syrah and Grenache. The Village Saint Gervais is a GSM blend, and Les Mourillons is 100% Syrah. Vinification is traditional, with the wines aged in concrete, except for the Syrah which is partly aged in barriques.

Château des Tours
153, route de Parisi, Quartier des Sablons, 84260 Sarrians
(33) 04 90 65 41 75
Emmanuel Reynaud
fax; (33) 04 90 65 38 46
chateaurayas.fr/vinsdestours.htm

⚠ ⛁

🍇 🚜 *40 ha; 165,000 bottles*
[map p. 80]

Owned by Emmanuel Reynaud, together with famed Château Rayas (see profile) in Châteauneuf-du-Pape, this property follows the same principles of reds based on Grenache harvested as ripe as possible. Production is 90% red; there are only 3 ha of white (both Grenache Blanc and Clairette). Reds come under IGP Vaucluse, Côtes du Rhône (65% Grenache, 15% Cinsault, and 20% Syrah), and Vacqueyras (80% Grenache and 20% Syrah). True to the tradition of Rayas, there are cuvées labeled "Réserve," under Côtes du Rhône and Vacqueyras. Under the halo of Château Rayas, the wines achieve extraordinary prices for their appellations: they are certainly very good, but perhaps not better than other top wines to the degree suggested by the price.

Domaine Chamfort
280 route Parandou - RD977, 84110 Sablet
(33) 04 90 46 94 75
Perdigao Vasco
domaine-chamfort@orange.fr
www.domaine-chamfort.fr

🚶 ⛁

🍇 🚜 *27 ha; 80,000 bottles*
[map p. 81]

Founded in 1960, the domain was run by Dennis Chamfort until he sold it in 2010 to Vasco Perdigao (originally Portuguese), who had previously worked in a cooperative but wanted to make his own wine. Vineyards are quite spread out, with 10 ha in Sarrians (part of Vacqueyras AOP), 4 ha in Rasteau, 5 ha in Sablet, and 6 ha which Vasco bought in Séguret in 2014. There is also a little IGP. Vacqueyras is the main production, and is a GSM; Rasteau and Sablet are blends of Grenache and Syrah, while Séguret is a blend of Grenache and Mourvèdre. All the wines are aged partly in concrete vat and part in large oak casks, but Vacqueyras also has 10% in barriques. There are also some special cuvées from plots of old vines. Vacqueyras Les 2 Louis is an equal blend of Grenache and Mourvèdre from 50-year-old vines; C'est Beau Là-Haut is a Séguret from a plot at 450m facing the Dentelles, and is 100% Grenache; and Les Patis is an IGP Vaucluse from 30-year old Syrah and Grenache. All the special cuvées are aged in oak.

Glossary of French Wine Terms

Classification
There are three levels of classification, but their names have changed:
- *AOP* (Appellation d'Origine Protégée, formerly AOC or Appellation d'Origine Contrôlée) is the highest level of classification. AOPs are tightly regulated for which grape varieties can be planted and for various aspects of viticulture and vinification.
- *IGP* (Indication Géographique Protegée, formerly Vin de Pays) covers broader areas with more flexibility for planting grape varieties, and few or no restrictions on viticulture and vinification.
- *Vin de France* (formerly Vin de Table) is the lowest level of classification and allows complete freedom with regards to varieties, viticulture, and vinification.
- *INAO* is the regulatory authority for AOP and IGP wines.

Producers
- *Domaine* on a label means the wine is produced only from estate grapes (the vineyards may be owned or rented).
- *Maison* on the label means that the producer is a negociant who has purchased grapes (or wine).
- *Negociants* may purchase grapes and make wine or may purchase wine in bulk for bottling themselves. Some negociants also own vineyards.
- *Cooperatives* buy the grapes from their members and make the wine to sell under their own label.

Growers
- There is no word for winemaker in French. The closest would be *oenologue*, meaning a specialist in vinification; larger estates (especially in Bordeaux) may have consulting oenologues.
- A *vigneron* is a wine grower, who both grows grapes and makes wine.
- A *viticulteur* grows grapes but does not make wine.
- A *régisseur* is the estate manager at a larger property, and may encompass anything from general management to taking charge of viticulture or (commonly) vinification.

Viticulture
- There are three types of viticulture where use of conventional treatments (herbicides, insecticides, fertilizers, etc.) is restricted:
- *Bio* is organic viticulture; certification is by AB France (Agriculture Biologique).

- *Biodynamique* is biodynamic viticulture, certified by Demeter.
- *Lutte raisonnée* means sustainable viticulture (using treatments only when necessary). There are various certifications including HVE (Haute Valeur Environmentale).

Winemaking

- *Vendange entière* means that whole clusters of grapes are used for fermentation.
- *Destemming* means that the grapes are taken off the stems and individual berries are put into the fermentation vat.
- *Remontage* (pump-over) means pumping up the fermenting wine from the bottom of the vat to spray over the cap of grape skins that forms on top of the fermenting wine.
- *Punch-down* means using a plunger to push the cap of grapes into the fermenting wine.
- *Cuvaison* is the period a wine spends in contact with the grape skins.
- *Battonage* describes stirring up the wine when it is aging (usually) in cask.
- *Élevage* is the aging of wine after fermentation has been completed.
- *Malo* is an abbreviation for malolactic fermentation, performed after the alcoholic fermentation, which reduces acidity. It's almost always done with red wines, and most often for non-aromatic white wines.
- A *vin de garde* is a wine intended for long aging.

Aging in oak

- A *fût* (*de chêne*) is an oak barrel of unspecified size.
- A *barrique* (in Bordeaux or elsewhere) has 225 liters or 230 liters (called a *pièce* in Burgundy).
- A *tonneau* is an old term for a 900 liter container, sometimes used colloquially for containers larger than barriques.
- A *demi-muid* is a 600 liter barrel.
- A *foudre* is a large wood cask, round or oval, from 20 hl to 100 hl.

Sweet wines

- *Moelleux* is medium-sweet wine.
- *Liquoreux* is fully sweet dessert wine.
- *Mutage* is addition of alcohol to stop fermentation and produce sweet wine.
- *Passerillage* leaves grapes on the vine for an extended period so that sugar concentration is increased by desiccation.

Index of Estates by Rating

3 star
Château de Beaucastel
Domaine de Beaurenard
Domaine Henri Bonneau
Château Rayas
Domaine du Vieux Télégraphe
2 star
Domaine Paul Autard
Château de la Gardine
Château La Nerthe
Clos des Papes
Domaine Roger Sabon
Domaine de La Solitude
Domaine Pierre Usseglio
1 star
Pierre Amadieu
Domaine Les Aphillanthes
Domaine des Bernardins
Domaine La Bouïssière
Domaine Brusset
Domaine Les Cailloux
Domaine du Cayron
Domaine le Clos des Cazaux
Domaine Chante Cigale
Domaine Chante Perdrix
Domaine Clos du Caillou
Domaine de Coyeux
Domaine de Durban
Domaine des Espiers
Château de la Font du Loup
Château Fortia
Domaine Gourt de Mautens
Domaine de La Janasse
Domaine de Marcoux
Martinelle
Clos du Mont-Olivet
Montirius
Domaine de Montvac
Domaine de La Mordorée
Château Mont-Redon
Domaine de L'Oratoire Saint-Martin
Domaine Les Pallières
Domaine du Pegau
Domaine Rabasse Charavin
Domaine Marcel Richaud
Château de Saint Cosme
Domaine Saint-Préfert
Domaine Le Sang des Cailloux
Domaine Santa-Duc
Château Sixtine
Domaine La Soumade
Maison Tardieu-Laurent
Château des Tourettes
Domaine de La Vieille Julienne
Domaine Le Vieux Donjon

Index of Organic and Biodynamic Estates

Domaine Alary
Domaine de l'Amauve
Domaine des Amouriers
Domaine Les Aphillanthes
Château de Beaucastel
Château Beauchêne
Domaine de Beaurenard
Domaine de la Charité
Domaine Charvin
Domaine Clos du Caillou
Domaine Coteaux Travers
Domaine de Cristia
Domaine des Espiers
Château de la Font du Loup
Domaine Giraud
Domaine Gourt de Mautens
Domaine de La Janasse
Clos du Joncuas
Domaine de Marcoux
Martinelle
Domaine de la Monardière
Montirius
Domaine de Montvac
Domaine de La Mordorée
Château La Nerthe
Domaine des Ondines
Domaine de L'Oratoire Saint-Martin
Domaine d'Ouréa
Clos des Papes
Domaine Rabasse Charavin
Domaine de La Réméjeanne
Mas des Restanques
Domaine Marcel Richaud
Château de Saint Cosme
Domaine Saint-Préfert
Domaine Le Sang des Cailloux
Domaine Santa-Duc
Domaine Raymond Usseglio
Domaine de La Vieille Julienne

Index of Estates by Appellation

Beaumes de Venise
Domaine des Bernardins
Domaine de Coyeux
Domaine de Durban

Châteauneuf-du-Pape
Domaine Paul Autard
Domaine du Banneret
Domaine de la Barroche
Château de Beaucastel
Domaine de Beaurenard
Domaine Henri Bonneau
Domaine Bosquet des Papes
Clos des Brusquières
Domaine Les Cailloux
Domaine Chante Cigale
Domaine Chante Perdrix
Domaine de la Charbonnière
Domaine Charvin
Domaine Clos du Caillou
Clos Saint Jean
Domaine de Cristia
Domaine Font de Michelle
Château de la Font du Loup
Château Fortia
Château de la Gardine
Domaine Giraud
Domaine de La Janasse
Domaine de Marcoux
Mas Saint-Louis
Clos du Mont-Olivet
Château Mont-Redon
Domaine de Nalys
Château La Nerthe
Ogier Cave des Papes
Clos de L'Oratoire des Papes
Clos des Papes
Domaine du Pegau
Domaine Pontifical

Château Rayas
Domaine Roger Sabon
Domaine Saint-Préfert
Château Sixtine
Domaine de La Solitude
Domaine Pierre Usseglio
Domaine Raymond Usseglio
Château de Vaudieu
Domaine de La Vieille Julienne
Domaine Le Vieux Donjon
Domaine du Vieux Télégraphe

Côtes du Rhône
Domaine des Amouriers
Domaine Les Aphillanthes
Domaine de la Charité
Montirius
Domaine des Ondines
Domaine de La Reméjeanne
Domaine Le Sang des Cailloux
Château des Tours

Côtes du Rhône Villages
Château Beauchêne
Domaine Cécile Chassagne
Maison Tardieu-Laurent

Côtes du Rhône Villages Cairanne
Domaine Alary
Domaine Brusset
Domaine de L'Oratoire Saint-Martin
Domaine Rabasse Charavin
Domaine Marcel Richaud

Côtes du Rhône Villages Laudun
Domaine Rouvre Saint-Léger

Côtes du Rhône Villages Sablet
Domaine de Piaugier
Domaine Chamfort

Côtes du Rhône Villages Séguret
Domaine de l'Amauve

Côtes du Rhône Villages St. Gervais
Domaine Sainte-Anne

Gigondas
Pierre Amadieu
Domaine des Bosquets
Domaine La Bouïssière
Domaine du Cayron
Domaine des Florets
Domaine de Font-Sane
Domaine les Goubert
Domaine du Grapillon d'Or
Clos du Joncuas
Maison Gabriel Meffre
Domaine Les Pallières
Domaine Raspail-Ay
Mas des Restanques
Château de Saint Cosme
Domaine Saint Gayan
Domaine Santa-Duc

Lirac
Château d'Aqueria

Lubéron
Château des Tourettes

Rasteau
Domaine Coteaux Travers
Domaine des Escaravailles
Domaine Gourt de Mautens
Domaine La Soumade

Tavel
Domaine de La Mordorée

Vacqueyras
Domaine le Clos des Cazaux
Domaine des Espiers
Domaine de la Monardière
Domaine de Montvac
Domaine d'Ouréa
Domaine les Semelles de Vent

Ventoux
Martinelle

Index of Estates by Name

Domaine Alary, 108
Pierre Amadieu, 67
Domaine de l'Amauve, 108
Domaine des Amouriers, 109
Domaine Les Aphillanthes, 82
Château d'Aqueria, 109
Domaine Paul Autard, 34
Domaine du Banneret, 98
Domaine de la Barroche, 98
Château de Beaucastel, 35
Château Beauchêne, 109
Domaine de Beaurenard, 37
Domaine des Bernardins, 68
Domaine Henri Bonneau, 38
Domaine Bosquet des Papes, 98
Domaine des Bosquets, 104
Domaine La Bouïssière, 69
Clos des Brusquières, 99
Domaine Brusset, 83
Domaine Les Cailloux, 39
Domaine du Cayron, 70
Domaine le Clos des Cazaux, 71
Domaine Cécile Chassagne, 110
Domaine Chante Cigale, 40
Domaine Chante Perdrix, 41
Domaine de la Charbonnière, 99
Domaine de la Charité, 110
Domaine Charvin, 99
Domaine Clos du Caillou, 42
Clos Saint Jean, 100
Domaine Coteaux Travers, 111
Domaine de Coyeux, 72
Domaine de Cristia, 100
Domaine de Durban, 73
Domaine des Escaravailles, 111
Domaine des Espiers, 74
Domaine des Florets, 104
Domaine Font de Michelle, 100
Château de la Font du Loup, 43
Domaine de Font-Sane, 104
Château Fortia, 44
Château de la Gardine, 45
Domaine Giraud, 101
Domaine les Goubert, 104
Domaine Gourt de Mautens, 84
Domaine du Grapillon d'Or, 105
Domaine de La Janasse, 47
Clos du Joncuas, 105
Domaine de Marcoux, 48
Martinelle, 96

Mas Saint-Louis, 101
Maison Gabriel Meffre, 105
Domaine de la Monardière, 106
Clos du Mont-Olivet, 49
Montirius, 85
Domaine de Montvac, 75
Domaine de La Mordorée, 86
Château Mont-Redon, 50
Domaine de Nalys, 102
Château La Nerthe, 52
Ogier Cave des Papes, 102
Domaine des Ondines, 111
Clos de L'Oratoire des Papes, 102
Domaine de L'Oratoire Saint-Martin, 87
Domaine d'Ouréa, 106
Domaine Les Pallières, 76
Clos des Papes, 53
Domaine du Pegau, 54
Domaine de Piaugier, 112
Domaine Pontifical, 103
Domaine Rabasse Charavin, 89
Domaine Raspail-Ay, 107
Château Rayas, 55
Domaine de La Réméjeanne, 90
Mas des Restanques, 107
Domaine Marcel Richaud, 91
Domaine Rouvre Saint-Léger, 112
Domaine Roger Sabon, 57
Château de Saint Cosme, 77
Domaine Saint Gayan, 107
Château Saint Roch, 112
Domaine Sainte-Anne, 113
Domaine Saint-Préfert, 58
Domaine Le Sang des Cailloux, 93
Domaine Santa-Duc, 79
Domaine les Semelles de Vent, 108
Château Sixtine, 59
Domaine de La Solitude, 60
Domaine La Soumade, 94
Maison Tardieu-Laurent, 95
Château des Tourettes, 97
Château des Tours, 113
Domaine Pierre Usseglio, 62
Domaine Raymond Usseglio, 103
Domaine Chamfort, 113
Château de Vaudieu, 103
Domaine de La Vieille Julienne, 63
Domaine Le Vieux Donjon, 64
Domaine du Vieux Télégraphe, 65

Books by Benjamin Lewin MW

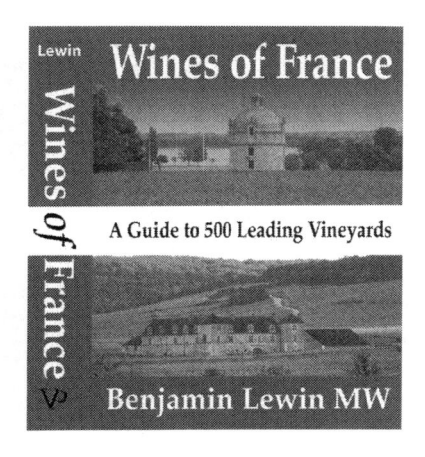

Wines of France

This comprehensive account of the vineyards and wines of France today is extensively illustrated with photographs and maps of each wine-producing area. Leading vineyards and winemakers are profiled in detail, with suggestions for wines to try and vineyards to visit.

Wine Myths and Reality

Extensively illustrated with photographs, maps, and charts, this behind-the-scenes view of winemaking reveals the truth about what goes into a bottle of wine. Its approachable and entertaining style immediately engages the reader in the wine universe.

In Search of Pinot Noir

Pinot Noir is a uniquely challenging grape with an unrivalled ability to reflect the character of the site where it grows. This world wide survey of everywhere Pinot Noir is grown extends from Burgundy to the New World, and profiles leading producers.

Claret & Cabs: The Story of Cabernet Sauvignon

This worldwide survey of Cabernet Sauvignon and its blends extends from Bordeaux through the New World, defines character of the wine from each region, and profiles leading producers.

Made in the USA
Middletown, DE
28 September 2018